W9-AFA-394

Ronald Reagan

All royalties from the sale of this book will benefit
The Ronald Reagan Presidential Library Foundation,
40 Presidential Drive, Simi Valley, California 93065
(805) 522-2977

RONALD REAGAN
THE GREAT COMMUNICATOR

EDITED BY FREDERICK J. RYAN, JR.

INTRODUCTION BY NANCY REAGAN
AFTERWORD BY PEGGY NOONAN

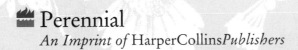

Perennial
An Imprint of HarperCollins*Publishers*

A hardcover edition of this book was published in 1995 by Collins Publishers San Francisco.

Ronald Reagan: The Great Communicator was produced by Tehabi Books, San Diego, California. Chris Capen, *President;* Tom Lewis, *Vice President of Development;* Andy Lewis, *Design Director;* Nancy Cash, *Editorial Director;* Sarah Morgans, *Editor;* Sébastien Loubert, *Art Director;* Laura Georgakakos, *Copy Editor;* Camille Cloutier, *Proofreader.*

Photography has been provided courtesy of The Ronald Reagan Presidential Library, The White House Staff Photographers, The Office of Ronald Reagan, and Peggy Grande. Supplemental photography has been provided by Digital Stock Professional (pages 26, 29, 56, 64), Scott Barrow (page 30), Kevin Halle (page 12), Robert Llewellyn (pages 15, 52, 71, 73, 96, 119, 124, 134), Joseph Sohm/ChromoSohm Media (pages 20, 41, 43, 108).

HarperCollins books may be purchased for educational, business, or sales promotional use. For information please write: Special Markets Department, HarperCollins Publishers Inc., 10 East 53rd Street, New York, NY 10022.

First Perennial edition published 2001.

The Library of Congress has catalogued the hardcover edition as follows:

Reagan, Ronald
    Ronald Reagan: the wisdom and humor of the Great Communicator / edited by Frederick J. Ryan Jr.
    p. cm.

ISBN 0-00-225121-3
    1. Reagan, Ronald—Quotations. 2. United States—Politics and government—1981-1989—Quotations, maxims, etc.
    I. Ryan, Frederick J. II. Title.
E838.5.R432 1995   95-15849
973.927'092—dc20   CIP

ISBN 0-06-093350-X (pbk.)

01 02 03 04 05 logo/QWK 10 9 8 7 6 5 4 3 2 1

The Ronald Reagan Presidential Foundation is a non-profit organization that funds the Ronald Reagan Presidential Library and Museum, the Center for Public Affairs, and the Presidential Learning Center, whose mission is to preserve President Reagan's legacy and to promote the timeless principles he championed: individual liberty, economic opportunity, global democracy, and national pride. Located in Simi Valley, California, the library houses 50 million pages of government documents and the museum is home to more than 100,000 artifacts that chronicle the life and legacy of America's 40th President. For more information, see our website at www.reaganfoundation.org.

TABLE OF CONTENTS

"I hope you are all Republicans," he said as he lay in the emergency room of The George Washington University Hospital. With an assassin's bullet just millimeters from his heart, President Ronald Reagan used his unique God-given skill to convey calm and assurance to those desperately working to save his life.

This episode revealed not only Reagan's incredible grace under pressure, but his unique ability to communicate warm humor in even the most dire circumstances.

His contagious optimism reignited a flickering national pride and inspired America to stand tall again. His impressive powers of persuasion convinced a Congress, comprised largely of the opposition party, to pass his economic proposals, leading to the greatest economic recovery in American history. His direct and honest approach in his dealings with America's adversaries reestablished our nation's strength as a world power to be reckoned with, and led to the crumbling of communism.

Throughout his nearly sixty years as a public figure, Ronald Reagan has maintained consistency in his views and values. Many of his speeches given decades ago ring as true today as they did when he first gave them. He did not adjust his beliefs to conform to prevailing political winds or to better fit someone else's view of political "correctness." Instead, he spoke directly from his heart to the hearts and minds of the American people. And, in so doing, he initiated the greatest love affair between an American President and his constituents in recent history.

In compiling this book, we reviewed thousands of speeches, statements, interviews, and press conferences—from Ronald Reagan's earliest public appearances through his post-presidential speeches. Many of the quotes recall Ronald Reagan's wonderful sense of humor and how often his use of levity relieved tensions and opened the door to discussion in difficult situations.

It is our hope that this book will serve students, political figures, and communicators everywhere for years to come. As did Ronald Reagan the man, may his words continue to inspire, enrich, and entertain the men and women of our great country and future generations of Americans.

PREFACE

This book would not have been possible without the tireless efforts of Erik Felten and Paul Wilkinson. They have reviewed every public utterance of the last fifty years by Ronald Reagan and have helped select the most appropriate excerpts for this book. Special thanks also to Peggy Grande, Cathy Busch, Eileen Foliente, Joanne Drake, Karen Moore, Bernadette Schurz, Eric Kowack, Brian Lee, Wendy Sparks, and Anne-Marie Behrendt for their special contributions to the book. And special appreciation to my wife, Genevieve McSweeney Ryan, for her support and encouragement on this project.

Frederick J. Ryan, Jr.

Throughout his years in public life, Ronnie spoke to groups small and large, at home and abroad. So many times when we were in public places, people would approach him and say how a particular one of his speeches had such deep personal meaning to them. Ronnie always did seem to have a very special way in which he "connected" with the American people. For Ronnie, speaking came naturally—he was never coached or trained how to speak, and I can't recall a time he was ever nervous before a speech or anxious after making one. He loved people and spoke to each person with heartfelt sincerity.

Ronnie has always been a basic man, simple in tastes but strong in his convictions. From his earliest political speeches to his final farewell to the American people, he has always been clear in his beliefs and consistent in his message.

Ronnie enjoyed writing his own speeches and did—at least until he became President, when time couldn't always allow it. But, even when in the White House, he personally penned his major addresses and worked closely with the staff in directing the themes and messages of his speeches. When he received a draft speech from his staff, he would often take it back to the living quarters of the White House in the evening. There he would carefully edit and add to it until it reflected the message he wished to deliver in the words he felt would best convey it.

Although his formal written speeches were always meaningful, I think many of his most memorable remarks were spontaneous statements and candid comments. They often demonstrated his grace under pressure, as well as his quick humor and clear thinking.

Today, for Ronald Reagan, the speeches have stopped but the words live on. Although Ronnie has begun what he called "the journey into the sunset" of his life, I believe his words and ideas will brighten America's skies and lift our national spirits for many generations to come. The wonderful selections in this book demonstrate the power of speech and Ronnie's unique ability to find just the right words for the occasion and see the world at its best. He has always been an optimist—not just in the good times when it's easy to be but in the tough times as well.

Today, the most important thing to me is to be with my husband. I am trying the best I can to finish the work that Ronnie began in building the Ronald Reagan Presidential Library. It has long been his hope that the Reagan Library be the place where his legacy lives on. I am so pleased that all the royalties from the sale of this book will go to supporting the activities of the Reagan Library.

Ronnie is a man that the country, and indeed the world, came to know and love. I thank God each day for bringing us together.

Nancy Reagan
Los Angeles, California, February 6, 2001

INTRODUCTION

While preparing to give a major presidential address to a television audience of millions, a staff member asked me what goes through my mind at such a time. With the audience sitting comfortably in their homes watching their television sets, I sit alone in my office looking into the dark lens of a camera. Just how do I connect with my audience?

I'll let you in on a little secret that dates back over fifty years to my first stint at a microphone. I was broadcasting sports for WHO Radio in Des Moines, Iowa. I had always dreamed of being a radio broadcaster, but I admit I was quite nervous the first time I sat alone in that small, windowless broadcasting room in front of a live microphone. How could I connect with all those people listening to the radio, I wondered? How could I converse with them in a natural way?

After a couple of stumbles and awkward silences it came to me. Many of the people listening were friends and acquaintances of mine. I wasn't talking to a group of faceless, unknown listeners. I could be talking over the radio to them the same way I would if we were face-to-face. I thought of the fellows in the local barber shop. I looked forward to my visit with them every two weeks when we'd swap jokes, talk sports, and tell stories while my hair was being cut. And I remembered that they always had the radio on and listened to just about every show that was broadcast.

So, sitting in that solitary booth, I started talking to the fellows in the barber shop the same way I did during our regular get-togethers.

I learned then the fundamental rule of public speaking, whether on the radio, on television, or to a live crowd: Talk to your audience, not over their heads or through them. Don't try to talk in a special language of broadcasting or even politics, just use normal everyday words.

Since those early days on radio, I have given more speeches than I ever dreamed. But I have never lost that vision of the fellows in the barber shop sitting around and listening to the radio. I've given enough speeches to practically fill the Ronald Reagan Presidential Library in Simi Valley, California and I am delighted that they have been used to assemble this book. I would like to convey my deep personal thanks to Fred Ryan and the team he put together to publish this book. I'm very pleased that it is a non-profit venture with all royalties going to the Ronald Reagan Presidential Library Foundation.

I'm not sure when I was first dubbed "The Great Communicator," but I have always been honored by that title. If I have in any way earned it, I hope it is because I have always tried to speak from the heart to you, the American people. God bless you for the privilege of allowing me to do so.

F ROM THE HEART

How can we not believe in the greatness of
America? How can we not do what is right and
needed to preserve this last best hope of man on
Earth? After all our struggles to restore America, to
revive confidence in our country, hope for our

VISIONS OF AMERICA

future—after all our hard-won victories earned
through the patience and courage of every citizen—
we cannot, must not, and will not turn back. We will
finish our job. How could we do less? We're
Americans.

State of the Union Address, January 25, 1988

Now we're standing inside this symbol of our democracy, and we see and hear again the echoes of our past: A general falls to his knees in the hard snow of Valley Forge; a lonely President paces the darkened halls and ponders his struggle to preserve the Union; the men of the Alamo call out encouragement to each other; a settler pushes west and sings a song, and the song echoes out forever and fills the unknowing air.

It is the American sound. It is hopeful, big-hearted, idealistic, daring, decent, and fair. That's our heritage, that's our song. We sing it still. For all our problems, our differences, we are together as of old. We raise our voices to the God who is the Author of this most tender music. And may He continue to hold us close as we fill the world with our sound—in unity, affection, and love—one people under God, dedicated to the dream of freedom that He has placed in the human heart, called upon now to pass that dream on to a waiting and hopeful world.

Inaugural Address, January 21, 1985

More than anything else, I want my candidacy to unify our country, to renew the American spirit and sense of purpose. I want to carry our message to every American, regardless of party affiliation, who is a member of the community of shared values.

From the Presidential Nomination Acceptance Address, Republican National Convention, Detroit, Michigan, July 17, 1980

You can play a special part in this future. You'll be its author: Take full advantage of the wonderful life that lies in store for you. Rejoice in your freedom, sample the full richness of the opportunities that lie before you. Help one another, trust in yourselves, and have faith in God, and you'll find more joy and happiness than you could imagine. And always remember that you are Americans, and it is your birthright to dream great dreams in this sweet and blessed land, truly the greatest, freest, strongest nation on Earth.

Remarks upon departure from the University of Virginia, Charlottesville, December 16, 1988

In America, our origins matter less than our destination, and that is what democracy is all about.

Address to the Republican National Convention, Houston, Texas, August 17, 1992

Good citizenship is vitally important if democracy is to survive and flourish. It means keeping abreast of the important issues of the day and knowing the stakes involved in the great conflicts of our time. It means bearing arms when necessary to fight for your country, for right, and for freedom. Good citizenship and defending democracy means living up to the ideals and values that make this country great. Today the world looks to America for leadership. They look to what they call our miracle economy for an answer to how they may give their people a better life. And they look to our courage and might to protect them from the forces of tyranny, brutality, and injustice.

Remarks to Marine Corps Basic Training Graduates, Parris Island, South Carolina, June 4, 1986

14

Loyalty, faithfulness, commitment, courage, patriotism, the ability to distinguish between right and wrong—I hope that these values are as much a part of your life as any calculus course or social science study. And so, do remember: Gratitude is a way to a deeper wisdom. Look for that deeper wisdom; believe me, there's a great hunger for it. And here you're in luck. As Americans, you have a special claim on it.

Remarks at the presentation ceremony for the Presidential Scholars Awards, June 16, 1988

This is the backbone of our country: Americans helping themselves, and each other. Reaching out and finding solutions—solutions that governments and huge institutions can't find.

National Charity Awards Dinner, Phoenix, Arizona, January 23, 1992

Remember this: When we come to the edge of our known world, we're standing on the shores of the infinite. Dip your hand in that limitless sea; you're touching the mystery of God's universe. Set sail across its waters and you embark on the boldest, most noble adventure of all. Out beyond our present horizons lie whole new continents of possibility, new worlds of hope waiting to be discovered. We've traveled far, but we've only begun our journey. There are hungry to feed, sicknesses to cure, and new worlds to explore. And this is no time for small plans or shrinking ambitions. We stand on the threshold of an epic age, an age of technological splendor and an explosion of human potential, an age for heroes. And I think I'm seeing many of them right here in this room.

Remarks to participants in the Young Astronauts Program, June 11, 1986

I got a letter from a man the other day, and I'll share it with you. This man said you can go to live in Turkey, but you can't become a Turk. You can go to live in Japan, but you cannot become Japanese— or Germany or France—and named all the others. But he said anyone from any corner of the world can come to America and become an American.

Remarks and Question and Answer Session with students at Suitland High School, Suitland, Maryland, January 20, 1988

Yes, he is first in our hearts and will be first for all time. But as Abraham Lincoln said, "To add brightness to the sun, or glory to the name of Washington, is … impossible. Let none attempt it … pronounce the name, and … leave it shining on."

Remarks at a Mount Vernon, Virginia, ceremony commemorating the 250th Anniversary of the birth of George Washington, February 22, 1982

Historians will make the final judgement about my years as Governor of California and as President of the United States, but personally, I feel good about what I have been able to accomplish, both in and out of government. My professional career has been varied. I have worked as a sportscaster, an actor, a labor leader, a lecturer, and a public official. This is something that is characteristic of the American way of life. The opportunity to advance oneself based on one's desires and abilities is a valued part of our existence and one to which I owe my success.

Written responses to questions submitted by the Soviet magazine Ogonek, *May 19, 1988*

17

Today vistas beyond imagination are being opened for humanity in space. A new future of freedom, both peaceful and bountiful, is being created. And America is telling the world: Follow us. We'll lead you there. This is the mission for which our nation itself was created, and we ask for God's guidance. America's as large as the universe, as infinite as space, as limitless as the vision and courage of her people.

Remarks congratulating the crew of the Space Shuttle Discovery, *October 14, 1988*

People from every race, culture, and creed on the face of the earth now inhabit this land. Their presence illuminates the basic yearning for freedom, peace, and prosperity that has always been the spirit of the New World.

Proclamation for Thanksgiving Day, 1988

Standing up for America also means standing up for the God who has so blessed this land. If we could just keep remembering that Moses brought down from the mountain the Ten Commandments, not ten suggestions—and if those of us who live for the Lord could remember that He wants us to love our Lord and our neighbor, then there's no limit to the problems we could solve or the mountains we could climb together as a mighty force for good.

The United States remains the last, best hope for a mankind plagued by tyranny and deprivation. America is no stronger than its people—and that means you and me. Well, I believe in you, and I believe that if we work together, then one day we will say, "We fought the good fight. We finished the race. We kept the faith." And to our children and our childrens' children we can say, "We did all that could be done in the brief time that was given us here on earth."

Remarks at the annual banquet of the National Rifle Association, Phoenix, Arizona, May 6, 1983

We've come to a moment in our history when party labels are unimportant. Philosophy is all important. Little men with loud voices cry doom, saying little is good in America. They create fear and uncertainty among us. Millions of Americans, especially our own sons and daughters, are seeking a cause they can believe in. There is a hunger in this country today—a hunger for spiritual guidance. People yearn once again to be proud of their country and proud of themselves, and to have confidence in themselves. And there's every reason why they should be proud. Some may have failed America, but America has never failed us, and there is so much to be proud of in this land.

Remarks at the Convention of Southern GOP, Atlanta, Georgia, December 7, 1973

18

19

My fondest hope is that your generation's voyage will be as momentous in peace as mine has been heroic in wars. At the height of World War II, Sir Winston Churchill reminded Britons that, "These are not dark days; these are great days—the greatest days our country has ever lived; and we must all thank God that we have been allowed, each of us according to our stations, to play a part in making these days memorable in the history of our race."

Oxford Union Society, "Democracy's Next Battle," Oxford, England, December 4, 1992

Presidents come and go. History comes and goes, but principles endure and insure future generations to defend liberty—not a gift from government, but a blessing from our Creator. Here, the lamp of individual conscience burns bright. By that I know we will all be guided to that dreamed-of day when no one wields a sword and no one drags a chain.

Presidential Medal of Freedom Ceremony, The White House, January 13, 1993

In the words of Thomas Paine: "These are times that try men's souls." We need more than summer soldiers and sunshine patriots. If we believe in principles of free enterprise that made our country great, we must stand up for them again today. We must draw anew on the individual strength, ingenuity, and vision that built America. But our gaze is not set on the past; it's firmly fixed on tomorrow. We must not mortgage our children's future to pay for the mistakes of today. The choice before our generation is grave, but clear: We must either face and solve our problems now or surrender to them forever.

Remarks at the Legislative Conference of the National Association of Realtors, March 29, 1982

This is the real task before us: To reassert our commitment as a nation to a law higher than our own, to renew our spiritual strength. Only by building a wall of such spiritual resolve can we, as a free people, hope to protect our own heritage and make it someday the birthright of all men.

Remarks at the annual Conservative Political Action Conference Dinner, March 20, 1981

Fellow Americans, our duty is before us tonight. Let us go forward, determined to serve selflessly a vision of man with God, government for people, and humanity at peace. For it is now our task to tend and preserve, through the darkest and coldest nights, that "sacred fire of liberty" that President Washington spoke of two centuries ago, a fire that tonight remains a beacon to all oppressed of the world, shining forth from this kindly, pleasant, greening land we call America.

Remarks at the annual Conservative Political Action Conference Dinner, February 26, 1982

21

Each new generation of Americans inherits as a birthright the legal protections secured, protected, and expanded by the vigilance and sacrifice of preceding generations. These rights—freedom of speech, trial by jury, personal liberty, a representative and limited government, and equal protection of the laws, to name but a few—give every citizen a vested interest in American justice.

Proclamation for Law Day USA, April 15, 1983

I've not taken your time this evening merely to ask you to trust me. Instead, I ask you to trust yourselves. That's what America is all about. Our struggle for nationhood, our unrelenting fight for freedom, our very existence—these have all rested on the assurance that you must be free to shape your life as you are best able to, that no one can stop you from reaching higher or take from you the creativity that has made America the envy of mankind.

Address to the Nation on Federal Tax Reduction Legislation, July 27, 1981

22

We the people: Starting the third century of a dream and standing up to some cynic who's been trying to tell us we're not going to get any better. Are we at the end? Well, I can't tell it any better than the real thing—a story recorded by James Madison from the final moments of the Constitutional Convention, September 17, 1787. As the last few members signed the document, Benjamin Franklin—the oldest delegate at 81 years and in frail health—looked over toward the chair where George Washington daily presided. At the back of the chair was painted the picture of a sun on the horizon.

Well, I know if we were there, we could see those delegates sitting around Franklin—leaning in to listen more closely to him. And then Dr. Franklin began to share his deepest hopes and fears about the outcome of their efforts, and this is what he said: "I have often looked at that picture behind the President without being able to tell whether it was a rising or setting sun: But now at length I have the happiness to know that it is a rising and not a setting sun." Well, you can bet it's rising because, my fellow citizens, America isn't finished. Her best days have just begun.

Address before a Joint Session of Congress on the State of the Union, January 27, 1987

Those who came to this untamed land brought family. And families built a nation. I'm convinced that today the majority of Americans want really what those first Americans wanted: A better life for themselves and their children, a minimum of government authority. Very simply, they want to be left alone in peace and safety to take care of the family by earning an honest dollar and putting away some savings. This may not sound too exciting, but there is a magnificence about it. On the farm, and on the street corner, in the factory and in the kitchen, millions of us ask nothing more, but certainly nothing less, than to live our own lives, according to our own values. At peace with ourselves, our neighbors, and the world.

National Television Address, July 6, 1976

Today we gather for a single purpose: To give the American people and the world a presidential library. There is, understandably, a great temptation to look back, to remember, to share warm and fond memories, and to reflect on the events which brought us here. And as we do, I hope we do not unduly focus on one man, one political party or even one country. Instead, our focus should be on the enduring fundamental principles of life that ennoble mankind.

Remarks during the dedication of the Ronald Reagan Presidential Library, November 4, 1991

I've spoken of the shining city all my political life, but I don't know if I ever quite communicated what I saw when I said it. But in my mind it was a tall, proud city built on rocks stronger than oceans, windswept, God-blessed, and teeming with people of all kinds living in harmony and peace; a city with free ports that hummed with commerce and creativity. And if there had to be city walls, the walls had doors and the doors were open to anyone with the will and heart to get here. That's how I saw it, and see it still.

Farewell Address to the Nation, January 11, 1989

24

There's still a lot of brush to clear out at the ranch, fences that need repair, and horses to ride. But I want you to know that if the fires ever dim, I'll leave my phone number and address behind just in case you need a foot soldier. Just let me know, and I'll be there, as long as words don't leave me and as long as this sweet country strives to be special during its shining moment on earth.

Remarks at the Republican National Convention,
New Orleans, Louisiana, August 15, 1988

Once during the campaign, I said, 'This is a wonderful time to be alive.' And I meant that. I meant that we're lucky not to live in pale and timid times. We've been blessed with the opportunity to stand for something—for liberty and freedom and fairness. And these are things worth fighting for, worth devoting our lives to. And we have good reason to be hopeful and optimistic.

We've made much progress already. So, let us go forth with good cheer and stout hearts—happy warriors out to seize back a country and a world to freedom.

Remarks at the annual Conservative Political Action Conference Dinner, March 1, 1985

I had a copy of the Soviet Constitution and I read it with great interest. And I saw all kinds of terms in there that sound just exactly like our own: "Freedom of assembly" and "freedom of speech" and so forth. Of course, they don't allow them to have those things, but they're in there in the constitution. But I began to wonder about the other constitutions—everyone has one—and our own, and why so much emphasis on ours. And then I found out, and the answer was very

simple. That's why you don't notice it at first, but it is so great that it tells the entire difference. All those other constitutions are documents that say that "We, the government, allow the people the following rights," and our Constitution says "We, the people, allow the government the following privileges and rights."

We give our permission to government to do the things that it does. And that's the whole story of the difference—why we're unique in the world and why no matter what our troubles may be, we're going to overcome all those troubles—and with your help and support because it's an ongoing process.

Remarks to delegates of the United States Senate Youth Program, February 5, 1981

This country was founded and built by people with great dreams and the courage to take great risks.

Remarks and a Question and Answer Session with members of the Massachusetts High Technology Council, Bedford, Massachusetts, January 26, 1983

I feel certain that, despite all the challenges that beset us, this nation of freedom will flourish. But if we're to succeed in the future, we must first learn our own past. We must learn to go to a building like this and hear the echoes and sense the greatness and draw strength. For to study American history is, in a sense, to study free will. It is to see that all our greatness has been built up by specific acts of choice and determination. And it is to see how very fragile our nation is, how very quickly so much that we cherish could be lost.

Remarks to volunteers and staff of "We the People," Philadelphia, Pennsylvania, April, 1, 1987

25

Voluntarism is an essential part of our plan to give the government back to the people. I believe the people are anxious for this responsibility. I believe they want to be enlisted in this cause. We have an unprecedented opportunity in America in these days ahead to build on our past traditions and the raw resources within our people. We can show the world how to construct a social system more humane, more compassionate, and more effective in meeting its members' needs than any ever known.

Remarks at the annual meeting of the National Alliance of Business, October 5, 1981

Our Founding Fathers envisioned a nation whose strength and vitality would emerge from the ingenuity of its people and their commitment to individual liberty. They understood that a nation's prosperity is dependent on the freedom of its citizens to pursue their hopes, dreams and creative ambitions. American entrepreneurs and small business owners enthusiastically embraced the challenges of freedom, and through the miracle of the marketplace, set in motion the forces of economic growth that made our nation uniquely productive. This pattern of economic development has inspired people throughout the world to look to America for a better life.

Proclamation for Small Business Week, March 7, 1983

I am no longer young. You might have suspected that. The house we hope to build is one that is not for my generation, but for yours. It is your future that matters. And I hope that when you're my age, you'll be able to say as I have been able to say: We lived in freedom, we lived lives that were a statement, not an apology.

Remarks to the students and faculty at St. John's University, New York, New York, March 28, 1985

27

Ladies and gentlemen, I'd planned to speak to you tonight to report on the State of the Union, but the events of earlier today have led me to change those plans. Today is a day for mourning and remembering. Nancy and I are pained to the core by the tragedy of the shuttle Challenger. We know we share this pain with all of the people of our country. This is truly a national loss.

Nineteen years ago, almost to the day, we lost three astronauts in a terrible accident on the ground. But we've never lost an astronaut in flight; we've never had a tragedy like this. And perhaps we've forgotten the courage it took for the crew of the shuttle. But they, the Challenger Seven, were aware of the dangers, but overcame them and did their jobs brilliantly. We mourn seven heroes: Michael Smith, Dick Scobee, Judith Resnik, Ronald McNair, Ellison Onizuka, Gregory Jarvis, and Christa McAuliffe. We mourn their loss as a nation together.

For the families of the seven, we cannot bear, as you do, the full impact of this tragedy. But we feel the loss, and we're thinking about you very much. Your loved ones were daring and brave, and they had that special grace, that special spirit

THE CHALLENGER DISASTER

that says, "Give me a challenge, and I'll meet it with joy." They had a hunger to explore the universe and discover its truths. They wished to serve, and they did. They served all of us. We've grown used to wonders in this century. It's hard to dazzle us. But for 25 years the United States space program has been doing just that. We've grown used to the idea of space, and perhaps we forget that we've only begun. We're still pioneers. They, the members of the Challenger crew, were pioneers.

And I want to say something to the schoolchildren of America who were watching the live coverage of the shuttle's takeoff. I know it is hard to understand, but sometimes painful things like this happen. It's all part of the process of exploration and discovery. It's all part of taking a chance and expanding man's horizons. The future doesn't belong to the fainthearted; it belongs to the brave. The Challenger crew was pulling us into the future, and we'll continue to follow them.

I've always had great faith in and respect for our space program, and what happened today does nothing to diminish it. We don't hide our space program. We don't keep secrets and cover things up. We do it all up front and in public. That's the way freedom is, and we wouldn't change it for a minute.

We'll continue our quest in space. There will be more shuttle flights and more shuttle crews and yes, more volunteers, more civilians, more teachers in space. Nothing ends here; our hopes and our journeys continue. I want to add that I wish I could talk to every man and woman who worked on this mission and tell them: "Your dedication and professionalism have moved and impressed us for decades. And we know your anguish. We share it."

There's coincidence today. On this day 390 years ago, the great explorer Sir Francis Drake died aboard ship off the coast of Panama. In his lifetime the great frontiers were the oceans, and an historian later said, "He lived by the sea, died on it, and was buried in it." Well, today we can say of the Challenger crew: Their dedication was, like Drake's, complete.

The crew of the space shuttle Challenger honored us by the manner in which they lived their lives. We will never forget them, nor the last time we saw them, this morning, as they prepared for their journey and waved goodbye and "slipped the surly bonds of earth," to "touch the face of God."

Address to the Nation
January 28, 1986

29

America has already succeeded where so many other historic attempts at freedom have failed. Already, we've made this cherished land the last best hope of mankind. It's up to us, in our generation, to carry on the hallowed task. It is up to us, however we may disagree on policies, to work together

THE FLAME OF FREEDOM

for progress and humanity so that our grandchildren, when they look back on us, can truly say that we not only preserved the flame of freedom, but cast its warmth and light further than those who came before us.

Remarks to the National Conference of Christians and Jews,
New York, New York, March 23, 1982

Freedom is a fragile thing and is never more than one generation away from extinction. It is not ours by inheritance; it must be fought for and defended constantly by each generation, for it comes only once to a people. Those who have known freedom, and then lost it, have never known it again.

First Inaugural Message as Governor of California, January 5, 1967

What I'm speaking of is a balance of safety, as opposed to a balance of terror. This is not only morally preferable, but it may result in getting rid of nuclear weapons altogether. It would be irresponsible and dangerous on our part to deny this promise to the world. And so we're dealing with the real issue of how to free the entire world from the nuclear threat. And this is why we want the Soviets to join us now in agreeing to equitable and verifiable reductions, and I mean significant reductions, in offensive nuclear arms.

Radio Address to the Nation on Soviet Strategic Defense Programs, October 12, 1985

Individual freedom and the profit motive were the engines of progress which transformed an American wilderness into an economic dynamo that provided the American people with a standard of living that is still the envy of the world.

Remarks at the National Space Club Luncheon, March 29, 1985

Now you may have heard the rumors to the effect that increasing government spending is not something I'm prone to do, and to tell the truth, there's a certain substance to these rumors. At the same time, I accept without question the words of George Washington: "To be prepared for war is one of the most effectual means of preserving peace." Now, in spite of some things you may have heard, he didn't tell me that personally. Still, I'm in full agreement and believe that he did say it.

But let me seriously speak about your employers. We've been through a period in which it seemed that we the people had forgotten that government is a convenience of, for, and by the people. And while we were busy with our

own affairs, government began to grow beyond the consent of the governed. Its growth was nourished by an ever-larger share of the people's earnings that it took by taxation which became more and more confiscatory. At the same time government neglected one of its prime responsibilities—national security—as it engaged more and more in social experimentation. Our margin of safety in an increasingly hostile world was allowed to diminish, and for a time it seemed that there was an erosion of respect for the honorable profession that you have chosen.

Address at the Commencement Exercises of the United States Military Academy, May 27, 1981

Freedom is the very essence of our nation. To be sure, ours is not a perfect nation. But even with our troubles, we remain the beacon of hope for oppressed peoples everywhere.

Never give up the fight for freedom—a fight which, though it may never end, is the most ennobling known to man.

Presentation of a section of the Berlin Wall, Ronald Reagan Presidential Library, April 12, 1990

To those neighbors and allies who share our freedom, we will strengthen our historic ties and assure them of our support and firm commitment. We will match loyalty with loyalty. We will strive for mutually beneficial relations. We will not use our friendship to impose on their sovereignty, for our own sovereignty is not for sale.

As for the enemies of freedom, those who are potential adversaries, they will be reminded that peace is the highest aspiration of the American people. We will negotiate for it, sacrifice for it; we will never surrender for it, now or ever.

Inaugural Address, January 20, 1981

We in America have learned bitter lessons from two world wars: It is better to be here ready to protect the peace than to take blind shelter across the sea, rushing to respond only after freedom is lost. We've learned that isolationism never was and never will be an acceptable response to tyrannical governments with an expansionist intent.

Ceremony commemorating the 40th Anniversary of the Normandy Invasion, June 6, 1984

I have often said that the tide of the future is a freedom tide. If so, it is also a peace tide, for the surest guarantee we have of peace is national freedom and democratic government.

Message to Congress on Freedom, Regional Security, and Global Peace, March 14, 1986

Our defense policy is based on a very simple premise: The United States will not start fights. We will not be the first to use aggression. We will not seek to occupy other lands or control other peoples. Our strategy is defensive; our aim is to protect the peace by ensuring that no adversaries ever conclude they could best us in a war of their own choosing.

Statement on United States Defense Policy, March 9, 1983

We desire peace. But peace is a goal, not a policy. Lasting peace is what we hope for at the end of our journey. It doesn't describe the steps we must take nor the paths we should follow to reach that goal.

Address to the Nation on Strategic Arms Reduction and Nuclear Deterrence, November 22, 1982

Q: On the summit, sir, British Prime Minister Margaret Thatcher met Mr. Gorbachev and said, "I like Mr. Gorbachev. We can do business together." Is it necessary, do you think, that you and Gorbachev like each other at the summit in order to do business?

A: Well, I wasn't going to give him a friendship ring or anything. No, seriously, I believe this. I think she made an observation out of this, and our own people who have been over there—our recent group of senators who met with him found him a personable individual. I'm sure I will too. It isn't necessary that we love or even like each other. It's only necessary that we are willing to recognize that for the good of the people we represent, on this side of the ocean and over there, that everyone will be better off if we can come to some decisions about the threat of war.

The President's News Conference, September 17, 1985

33

Working for peace is both a moral duty and a practical necessity. We should have no illusions. This task is immensely difficult, and we can no more solve the world's problems than we can isolate ourselves from them. But the search for peace is the surest way to preserve all that we cherish and avoid the nightmares that we fear.

Remarks at the Chamber of Commerce of the United States, April 26, 1982

One thing is certain. If we're to continue to advance world peace and human freedom, America must remain strong. We must turn a deaf ear to those born-again patriots who talk about strength while serving up the same old menu of weakness. If we have learned anything these last eight years, it's that peace through strength works.

Radio Address to the Nation on Foreign Policy, September 24, 1988

Since the founding of our Armed Forces during the Revolutionary War, our country has always done without large standing armies and navies. Our great success story—unique in history—has been based on peaceful achievements in every sphere of human experience. In our two centuries of continuous democracy, we've been the envy of the world in technology, commerce, agriculture, and economic potential.

Our status as a free society and world power is not based on brute strength. When we've taken up arms, it has been for the defense of freedom for ourselves and for other peaceful nations who needed our help. But now, faced with the development of weapons with immense destructive power, we've no choice but to maintain ready defense forces that are second to none. Yes the cost is high, but the price of neglect would be infinitely higher.

Remarks at the Recommissioning Ceremony for the U.S.S. New Jersey, Long Beach, California, December 28, 1982

My mission, stated simply, is a mission for peace. It is to engage the new Soviet leader in what I hope will be a dialog for peace that endures beyond my presidency. It is

to sit across from Mr. Gorbachev and try to map out, together, a basis for peaceful discourse even though our disagreements on fundamentals will not change. It is my fervent hope that the two of us can begin a process which our successors and our people can continue—facing our differences frankly and openly and beginning to narrow and resolve them; communicating effectively so that our actions and intentions are not misunderstood; and eliminating the barriers between us and cooperating wherever possible for the greater good of all.

Address to the Nation on the upcoming Soviet-United States Summit Meeting in Geneva, Switzerland, November 14, 1985

You may think this a little mystical, and I've said it many times before, but I believe there was a divine plan to place this great continent here between the two oceans to be found by peoples from every corner of the Earth. I believe we were preordained to carry the torch of freedom for the world.

Heritage Foundation Annual Board Meeting, Carmel, California, June 22, 1990

34

There is one sign the Soviets can make that would be unmistakable, that would advance dramatically the cause of freedom and peace. General Secretary Gorbachev, if you seek peace, if you seek prosperity for the Soviet Union and Eastern Europe, if you seek liberalization: Come here to this gate! Mr. Gorbachev, open this gate! Mr. Gorbachev, tear down this wall!

Remarks at the Brandenburg Gate, West Berlin, Germany, June 12, 1987

Let us begin with candor, with words that rest on plain and simple facts. The differences between America and the Soviet Union are deep and abiding. The United States is a democratic nation. Here the people rule. We build no walls to keep them in, nor organize any system of police to keep them mute. We occupy no country. The only land abroad we occupy is land beneath the graves where our heroes rest. What is called the West is a voluntary association of free nations, all of whom fiercely value their independence and their sovereignty. And as deeply as we cherish our beliefs, we do not seek to compel others to share them.

Address to the United Nations General Assembly, New York, New York, October 24, 1985

All of these things—learning to control the government, limiting the amount of money it can take from us, protecting our country through a strong defense—all of these things revolve around one word, and that word is "freedom."

Remarks at the annual convention of National Religious Broadcasters, February 4, 1985

The task that has fallen to us as Americans is to move the conscience of the world, to keep alive the hope and dream of freedom. For if we fail or falter, there'll be no place for the world's oppressed to flee to. This is not the role we sought. We preach no manifest destiny. But like the Americans who brought a new nation into the world 200 years ago, history has asked much of us in our time. Much we've already given, much more we must be prepared to give.

Remarks at the annual Conservative Political Action Conference Dinner, February 18, 1983

In December 1979, the Soviet Union invaded Afghanistan without provocation and with overwhelming force. Since that time, the Soviet Union has sought, through every available means, to assert its control over Afghanistan.

The Afghan people have defied the Soviet Union and have resisted with a vigor that has few parallels in modern history. The Afghan people have paid a terrible price in their fight for freedom. Their villages and homes have been destroyed; they have been murdered by bullets, bombs, and chemical weapons.

One-fifth of the Afghan people have been driven into exile. Yet their fight goes on. The international community, with the United States joining governments around the world, has condemned the invasion of Afghanistan as a violation of every standard of decency and international law and has called for a withdrawal of the Soviet troops from Afghanistan.

Proclamation for Afghanistan Day, March 10, 1982

If I can leave the young people of Europe with one message, it is this: History is on the side of the free. Hope and an unshakable belief in our basic values of freedom and human rights—these are the only guides we need as we travel into not only the 21st Century but the third millennium. The crisis of confidence in the West a decade ago has been replaced by strength and assurance.

Address to Western Europe from the Venice Economic Summit, June 5, 1987

37

When Brezhnev first became President, he invited his elderly mother to come up and see his suite of offices in the Kremlin and then put her in his limousine and drove her to his fabulous apartment there in Moscow. And in both places, not a word. She looked; she said nothing. Then he put her in his helicopter and took her out to the country home outside Moscow in a forest. And, again, not a word. Finally, he put her in his private jet and down the shores of the Black Sea to see that marble palace which is known as his beach home. And finally she spoke. She said, "Leonid, what if the communists find out?"

Remarks at the Eureka College Alumni Association Dinner, Eureka, Illinois, May 9, 1982

When was the last time you bought a car—or there are some other things there—even a good cheese or videocassette recorder and the label read, "Made in the U.S.S.R.?"

Remarks at the annual convention of the National Association of Counties, Indianapolis, Indiana, July 13, 1987

In the 2,765 days of our administration, not one inch of ground has fallen to the communists.

Remarks at the Republican National Convention, New Orleans, Louisiana, August 15, 1988

We Americans make no secret of our belief in freedom. In fact it's something of a national pastime. Every four years the American people choose a new President, and 1988 is one of those years. At one point there were 13 major candidates running in the two major parties, not to mention all the others, including the socialist and libertarian candidates, all trying to get my job. About 1,000 local television stations, and 1,700 daily newspapers, each one an independent private enterprise, fiercely independent of the government, report on the candidates, grill them in interviews, and bring them together for debates. In the end, the people vote; they decide who will be the next President. But freedom doesn't begin or end with elections.

Remarks at a Question and Answer Session with the students and faculty at Moscow State University, May 31, 1988

History demonstrates that time and again, in place after place, economic growth and human progress make the greatest strides in countries that encourage economic freedom.

Government has an important role in helping to develop a country's economic foundation. But the critical test is whether government is genuinely working to liberate individuals by creating incentives to work, save, invest, and succeed.

Individual farmers, laborers, owners, traders, and managers—they are the heart and soul of development. Trust them. Because whenever they are allowed to create and build, wherever they are given a personal stake in deciding economic policies and benefiting from their success, then societies become more dynamic, prosperous, progressive, and free.

With sound understanding of our domestic freedom and responsibilities, we can construct effective international cooperation. Without it, no amount of international good will and action can produce prosperity.

Statement at the First Plenary Session of the International Meeting on Cooperation and Development, Cancun, Mexico, October 22, 1981

38

I am a collector of stories that I can establish are actually told by the people of the Soviet Union among themselves. And this one has to do with the fact that in the Soviet Union, if you want to buy an automobile, there is a 10-year wait. And you have to put the money down ten years before you get the car. So, there was a young fellow there that had finally made it, and he was going through all the bureaus and agencies that he had to go through, and signing all the papers, and finally got to the last agency where they put the stamp on it. And then he gave them his money, and they said, "Come back in ten years and get your car." And he said, "Morning or afternoon?" And the man that had put the stamp on says, "Well, wait a minute," he says, "we're talking about ten years from now. What difference does it make?" He said, "The plumber is coming in the morning."

Remarks at a Fundraising Reception for Senator Orrin Hatch of Utah, June 17, 1987

We who live in free market societies believe that growth, prosperity and, ultimately, human fulfillment are created from the bottom up, not the government down. Only when the human spirit is allowed to invent and create, only when individuals are given a personal stake in deciding economic policies and benefiting from their success—only then can societies remain economically alive, dynamic, prosperous, progressive, and free.

Trust the people. This is the one irrefutable lesson of the entire postwar period, contradicting the notion that rigid government controls are essential to economic development. The societies which have achieved the most spectacular broad-based economic progress in the shortest period of time are not the most tightly controlled, not necessarily the biggest in size, or the wealthiest in natural resources. No, what unites them all is their willingness to believe in the magic of the marketplace.

Everyday life confirms the fundamentally human and democratic ideal that individual effort deserves an economic reward. Nothing is more crushing to the spirit of working people and to the vision of development itself than the absence of reward for honest toil and legitimate risk. So let me speak plainly: We cannot have prosperity and successful development without economic freedom; nor can we preserve our personal and political freedoms without economic freedom.

Governments that set out to regiment their people with the stated objective of providing security and liberty have ended up losing both. Those which put freedom as the first priority find they have also provided security and economic progress.

Remarks at the annual meeting of the Board of Governors of the World Bank Group and International Monetary Fund, September 29, 1981

It's no secret that I wear a hearing aid. Well, just the other day, all of a sudden, it went haywire. We discovered the KGB had put a listening device in my listening device.

Remarks at The White House Correspondents Association Annual Dinner, April 22, 1987

And, Billy [Graham], I'm going to have to tell them something that you told me, because with all this, too, there is a practical side of life. Reverend Graham was in the Soviet Union and invited by a bureaucrat of that governmental structure to lunch, and found himself faced with a lunch, as he described it, that was more magnificent and more of a gourmet type of thing than he had ever seen—caviar that wouldn't stop and every other thing that you could eat. And he couldn't resist saying to his host, "But how can you live this way, do this, when there are so many people out there in your country that don't have enough to eat, that are hungry?" And the man said, "I worked hard for this." And, God bless him, Billy Graham said, "That's what the capitalists say."

Remarks at the Presentation Ceremony for the Presidential Medal of Freedom, February 23, 1983

A broader reading of history shows that appeasement, no matter how it is labeled, never fulfills the hopes of the appeasers.

Address to Cambridge Union Society, Cambridge, England, December 5, 1990

Two Soviets … were talking to each other. And one of them asked, "What's the difference between the Soviet Constitution and the United States Constitution?" And the other one said, "That's easy. The Soviet Constitution guarantees freedom of speech and freedom of gathering. The American Constitution guarantees freedom after speech and freedom after gathering."

Remarks to community leaders in New Britain, Connecticut, July 8, 1987

I consider it a tragedy that at some campuses in my own country, those who hold unfashionable ideas are hooted off the stage, or denied a forum in the first place. What a travesty on intellectual inquiry; what a perversion of the great chaotic, yet essential, marketplace of ideas that we call democracy. But then, I have always believed, at home and abroad, that the only cure for what ails democracy is more democracy.

Remarks to Oxford Union Society, Oxford, England, December 4, 1992

This is our dilemma, and it's a profound one. We must both defend freedom and preserve the peace. We must stand true to our principles and our friends while preventing a holocaust.

The Western commitment to peace through strength has given Europe its longest period of peace in a century. We cannot conduct ourselves as if the special danger of nuclear weapons did not exist. But we must not allow ourselves to be paralyzed by the problem, to abdicate our moral duty. This is the challenge history has left us.

Remarks and a Question and Answer Session at the Los Angeles World Affairs Council Luncheon, March 31, 1983

I believe that the most essential element of our defense of freedom is our insistence on speaking out for the cause of religious liberty.

Remarks at Conference on Religious Liberty, April 16, 1985

Let it never be said of this generation of
Americans that we became so obsessed with
failure that we refused to take risks that
could further the cause of peace and
freedom in the world.

*Address before a Joint Session of Congress on the
State of the Union, January 27, 1987*

We don't have to stretch our memories back too far to remember that the American people twice, by overwhelming majorities, voted clearly and emphatically for something that all of us here believe in: They voted for peace in the only way it can ever be secured; they voted for peace through strength.

Remarks at the annual Leadership Conference of the American Legion, February 29, 1988

Terrorism is the preferred weapon of weak and evil men. And as Edmund Burke reminded us, in order for evil to succeed, it's only necessary that good men do nothing. Yesterday we demonstrated once again that doing nothing is not America's policy; it's not America's way. America's policy has been and remains to use force only as a last … resort. We would prefer not to have to repeat the events of last night. What is required is for Libya to end its pursuit of terror for political goals. The choice is theirs.

Remarks at a White House Meeting with members of the American Business Conference, April 15, 1986

Let us be frank. Evil still stalks the planet. Its ideology may be nothing more than bloodlust; no program more complex than economic plunder or military aggrandizement. But it is evil all the same. And wherever there are forces that would destroy the human spirit and diminish human potential, they must be recognized and they must be countered.

Oxford Union Society, "Democracy's Next Battle," Oxford, England, December 4, 1992

I have openly expressed my view of the Soviet system. I don't know why this should come as a surprise to Soviet leaders, who have never shied from expressing their view of our system. But this doesn't mean that we can't deal with each other. We don't refuse to talk when the Soviets call us imperialist aggressors and worse, or because they cling to the fantasy of a communist triumph over democracy. The fact that neither of us likes the other system is no reason to refuse to talk.

Address to the Nation and other countries on United States-Soviet Relations, January 16, 1984

I'd always believed in the importance of peace through strength. And the military is the provider of that strength. So we must equip them, train them and support them. Over the years, American military leadership has brought us to even greater heights than we could ever imagine. In times of peace and in times of war, America's military power has lead our nation to many great victories.

Presentation of the 1993 Ronald Reagan Freedom Award, November 9, 1993

Progress is not foreordained. The key is freedom: Freedom of thought, freedom of information, freedom of communication.

Remarks at a Question and Answer Session with the students and faculty at Moscow State University, May 31, 1988

I believe that communism is another sad, bizarre chapter in human history whose last pages even now are being written. I believe this because the source of our strength in the quest for human freedom is not material, but spiritual. And because it knows no limitation, it must terrify and ultimately triumph over those who would enslave their fellow man. For in the words of Isaiah: "He giveth power to the faint; and to them that have no might He increases strength .... But they that wait upon the Lord shall renew their strength; they shall mount up with wings as eagles; they shall run, and not be weary."

Remarks at the annual convention of the National Association of Evangelicals, Orlando, Florida, March 8, 1983

Life and the preservation of freedom to live it in dignity is what we are on this earth to do.

Address to the United Nations General Assembly, New York, New York, October 24, 1985

It seems that they were having some trouble with speeders in the Soviet Union, even though they don't have any automobiles. So, an order was issued that everybody, no matter who it was, caught speeding got a ticket. And one day General Secretary Gorbachev was coming out of his country home. He's late getting to the Kremlin. So, he told his driver to get in the backseat and he'd drive. And down the road he went, past two motorcycle policemen. One of them took out after him. In just a few minutes, he was back with his buddy. And the buddy said, "Well, did you give him a ticket?" And he said, "No." He said, "You didn't? Why not? We're supposed to give everyone a ticket." He said, "No, he was too important." "But," he said, "who was it?" "Well," he said, "I couldn't recognize him. But his driver was Gorbachev."

Remarks following a visit to the Reynolds Metals Company, Richmond, Virginia, March 28, 1988

The story is told that one night at dinner here at Mount Vernon, Lafayette said to Washington, "General, you Americans even in war and desperate times have a superb spirit. You're happy and you're confident. Why is it?" And Washington answered, "There is freedom. There is space for a man to be alone and think, and there are friends who owe each other nothing but affection."

Remarks at a Mount Vernon, Virginia, ceremony commemorating the 250th Anniversary of the birth of George Washington, February 22, 1982

The Declaration of Independence and the Constitution of these United States are covenants we have made not only with ourselves, but with all mankind. Our founding documents proclaim to the world that freedom is not the sole perogative of a chosen few. It is the universal right of all God's children.

Remarks to the Captive Nations Week Conference, Los Angeles, California, July 15, 1991

44

Those nations and states which have secured man's highest aspirations for freedom, opportunity and justice, have always been those willing to trust their people, confident that their skills and their talents are equal to any challenge.

Address as Governor of California, 1974

Having a little bit of freedom is like being a little bit pregnant. It isn't possible. One must be entirely free to think bold—even heretical—thoughts and to communicate them. And, one must be free to acquire information from any source. A great tide of information flows into and out of the Soviet Union today and that is good. It is good for those of you who are now exercising new freedoms and it's good for us outside your land, for communication between peoples has the effect of reducing stereotypes to realities.

Address in Moscow, September 27, 1990

It was the British historian Arnold Toynbee who defined life as a voyage of discovery and not a safe harbor. How true. After a lifetime spanning most of this tumultuous century, my voyage is drawing to a close. It has been an extraordinary trip by any standard.

With my own eyes, I have witnessed the birth of communism and the death of communism. I have seen the rise and fall of Nazi tyranny, the subsequent cold war and the nuclear nightmare that for fifty years haunted the dreams of children everywhere. During that time, my generation defeated totalitarianism, and more recently we have begun to destroy the weapons of mass destruction. As a result, your world is poised for better tomorrows. What will you do on your journey?

As I see it, you have the opportunity to set and enforce international standards of civilized behavior. Does that sound unrealistic? It is part of the great legacy of Oxford that rings down through the centuries—the power to effect change when it is needed and the wisdom to resist change when it is unwise.

Oxford Union Society, "Democracy's Next Battle," Oxford, England, December 4, 1992

Two visions of the world remain locked in dispute. The first believes all men are created equal by a loving God who has blessed us with freedom. Abraham Lincoln spoke for us: "No man," he said, "is good enough to govern another without the other's consent."

The second vision believes that religion is opium for the masses. It believes that eternal principles like truth, liberty, and democracy have no meaning beyond the whim of the state. And Lenin spoke for them: "It is true, that liberty is precious," he said, "so precious that it must be rationed."

Well, I'll take Lincoln's version over Lenin's—and so will citizens of the world if they're given free choice.

Remarks at a ceremony marking the annual observance of Captive Nations Week, July 19, 1983

It's our earnest prayer to serve America in peace. It's our solemn commitment to defend her in a time of war.

Remarks at the U.S. Coast Guard Academy Commencement Ceremony, New London, Connecticut, May 18, 1988

45

As is always the case, once people who have been deprived of basic freedom taste a little if it, they want all of it. It was as if Gorbachev had uncorked a magic bottle and a genie floated out, never to be put back again. Glasnost was that genie.

Address to Cambridge Union Society, Cambridge, England, December 5, 1990

In Russia and the other new states, democracy is flourishing. Churches and synagogues are opening. Newspapers are publishing. Citizens wishing to emigrate are allowed to leave. Troops have come home from places where they did not belong. Private businesses are springing up in previously unimaginable places.

Remarks at a presentation of the Freedom Award to Mikhail Gorbachev, Ronald Reagan Presidential Library, May 4, 1992

And may I conclude with a little Irish blessing—although, some suggest it's a curse: May those who love us, love us. And those who don't love us, may God turn their hearts. And if He doesn't turn their hearts, may He turn their ankles so we'll know them by their limping.

Remarks on Administration Goals to Senior Presidential Appointees, September 8, 1987

46

So far détente's been a one-way street that the Soviet Union has used to pursue its own aims. Their goal must be the promotion of world revolution and a one-world socialist or communist state, whichever word you want to use. Now as long as they do that and as long as they, at the same time, have openly and publicly declared that the only morality they recognize is what will further their own cause ... you keep that in mind.

The President's News Conference, January 29, 1981

I don't know all the national anthems of the world, but I do know this: The only anthem of those I do know that ends with a question is ours, and may it be ever thus. Does that banner still wave "o'er the land of the free and the home of the brave?" Yes, it does, and we're going to see that it continues to wave over that kind of a country.

Remarks at the Republican Congressional "Salute to President Ronald Reagan" Dinner, May 4, 1982

But with regard to the Soviet Union ... [w]hat is being called a hard line, I think is realism. I had some experience with communists—not of the Soviet kind, but domestic, in our own country, some years ago when I was president of a labor union there.

Interview with representatives of NHK Television, Tokyo, Japan, November 11, 1983

Every lesson of history tells us that appeasement does not lead to peace. It invites an aggressor to test the will of a nation unprepared to meet that test. And tragically, those who seemingly want peace the most, our young people, pay the heaviest price for our failure to maintain our strength.

Address as Governor of California, 1972

My favorite cartoon of the last few years was one—right after we really began rebuilding our military—of two Russian generals. And one of them was saying to the other, "I liked the arms race better when we were the only ones in it."

Remarks at White House briefing for Administration supporters, June 29, 1987

In this land occurred the only true revolution in man's history. All other revolutions simply exchanged one set of rulers for another. Here for the first time the Founding Fathers—that little band of men so advanced beyond their time that the world has never seen their like since—evolved a government based on the idea that you and I have the God-given right and ability within ourselves to determine our own destiny. Freedom is never more than one generation away from extinction. We didn't pass it on to our children in the bloodstream. It must be fought for, protected, and handed on for them to do the same, or one day we will spend our sunset years telling our children and our children's children what it was once like in the United States when men were free.

Annual meeting of the Phoenix Chamber of Commerce, March 30, 1961

47

Our national purpose is to unleash the full talent and genius of the individual, not to create mass movements with the citizenry subjecting themselves to the whims of the state. Here, as nowhere in the world, we are established to provide the ultimate in freedom consistent with law and order.

Remarks at Eureka College, Eureka, Illinois, September 28, 1967

It's been years since I stood at the Brandenburg Gate and called for the Wall to come down. It wasn't merely a polite suggestion. I was angry, because as I looked over the Wall into East Germany, I could see the people being kept away— their government didn't want them to hear what we were saying. But I think that they knew what we were saying and they wanted a better life.

Presentation of a section of the Berlin Wall, Ronald Reagan Presidential Library, April 12, 1990

We are now approaching an extremely important phase in East-West relations as the current Soviet leadership is succeeded by a new generation. Both the current and new Soviet leadership should realize aggressive policies will meet a firm Western response. On the other hand, a Soviet leadership devoted to improving its people's lives, rather than expanding its armed conquests, will find a sympathetic partner in the West. The West will respond with expanded trade and other forms of cooperation. But all this depends on Soviet actions. Standing in the Athenian marketplace 2,000 years ago, Demosthenes said, "What sane man would let another man's words rather than his deeds proclaim who is at peace and who is at war with him?"

Peace is not the absence of conflict, but the ability to cope with conflict by peaceful means. I believe we can cope. I believe that the West can fashion a realistic, durable policy that will protect our interests and keep the peace, not just for this generation but for your children and your grandchildren.

Commencement Address, Eureka College, Illinois, May 9, 1982

The dustbin of history is littered with the remains of those countries which relied on diplomacy to secure their freedom. We must never forget … in the final analysis … that it is our military, industrial and economic strength that offers the best guarantee of peace for America in times of danger.

Address as Governor of California, 1974

The principles of wealth creation transcend time, people, and place. Governments which deliberately subvert them by denouncing God, smothering faith, destroying freedom, and confiscating wealth have impoverished their people. Communism works only in heaven, where they don't need it, and in hell, where they've already got it.

Remarks at the National Conference of the National Federation of Independent Business, June 22, 1983

The United States is a natural athlete. No nation can claim all the advantages of America—population size, national resources, political stability, productive capacity, military strength, technological genius, cultural influence. We are a nation that finds change and innovation to be a tonic.

Remarks in Osaka, Japan,
October 28, 1989

Before I took up my current line of work, I got to know a thing or two about negotiating when I represented the Screen Actors Guild in contract talks with the studios. After the studios, Gorbachev was a snap.

Remarks to the National Chamber
Foundation, November 17, 1988

We're still Jefferson's children, still believers that freedom is the unalienable right of all of God's children. It's so precious, yet freedom is not something that can be touched, heard, seen, or smelled. It surrounds us, and if it were not present, as accustomed to it as we are, we would be alarmed, overwhelmed by outrage, or perhaps struck by a sense of being smothered. The air we breathe is also invisible and taken for granted, yet if it is denied even for a few seconds, we realize instantly how much it means to us. Well, so too with freedom.

Freedom is not created by government, nor is it a gift from those in political power. It is, in fact, secured more than anything else by those limitations I mentioned that are placed on those in government.

Remarks announcing America's Economic
Bill of Rights, July 3, 1987

49

The Soviet Union with all its military might, with its massive subsidy of the Cuban economy, can't make the system produce anything but repression and terror. It reminds me of the story—I happen to collect stories that the Soviet people are telling each other, the Russian people. It indicates their cynicism with their own system. This is a story of a commissar who visited one of their collective farms, and he stopped the first farmer that he met, and he asked about life on the farm. And the man said, "It's wonderful. I've never heard anyone complain about anything since I've been here." And the commissar then said, "Well, what about the crops?" "Oh," he said, "the crops are wonderful." "What about the potatoes?" "Oh, sir," he said, "the potatoes, there are so many that if we put them in one pile they would touch the foot of God." And the commissar said, "Just a minute. In the Soviet Union there is no God." And the farmer said, "Well, there are no potatoes either."

Remarks at a Cuban Independence Day celebration, Miami, Florida, May 20, 1983

There seems to be an increasing awareness of something we Americans have known for some time: That the ten most dangerous words in the English language are, "Hi, I'm from the Government, and I'm here to help."

Remarks to representatives of the Future Farmers of America, July 28, 1988

Despite the spread of democracy and capitalism, human nature has not changed. It is still an unpredictable mixture of good and evil. Our enemies may be irrational, even outright insane—driven by nationalism, religion, ethnicity or ideology. They do not fear the United States for its diplomatic skills or the number of automobiles and software programs it produces. They respect only the firepower of our tanks, planes, and helicopter gunships.

Remarks at Commencement Exercises, The Citadel, May 15, 1993

The hope of human freedom—the quest for it, the achievement of it—is the American saga. And I've often recalled one group of early settlers making a treacherous crossing of the Atlantic on a small ship when their leader, a minister, noted that perhaps their venture would fail and they would become a byword, a footnote to history. But perhaps, too, with God's help, they might also found a new world, a city upon a hill, a light unto nations.

Final Radio Address to the Nation, January 14, 1989

Bismarck reflected once that the supreme fact of the 19th Century was that Great Britain and the United States shared the same language. And surely future historians will note that a supreme fact of this century was that Great Britain and the United States shared the same cause; the cause of human freedom.

Remarks at the Welcoming Ceremony for British Prime Minister Margaret Thatcher, November 16, 1988

50

As most of you know, Margaret and I go back quite a ways. We met at a time before she became Prime Minister and I became President. From the moment we met, we discovered that we shared quite similar views of government and freedom. Margaret ended our first meeting by telling me, "we must stand together," and that's exactly what we've done in the years since—as friends and as political allies. Margaret Thatcher is one of the giants of our century. Her many achievements will be appreciated more and more as time goes on and history is written. For me, she has been a staunch ally, my political soulmate, a great visionary, and dear, dear friend.

Remarks at the Republican National Committee's 1994 Gala on the occasion of Ronald Reagan's 83rd Birthday, Washington, D.C., February 3, 1994

Our government has no power except that granted it by the people. It is time to check and reverse the growth of government, which shows signs of having grown beyond the consent of the governed.

It is my intention to curb the size and influence of the federal establishment and to demand recogni-

PEOPLE ARE THE GOVERNMENT

tion of the distinction between the powers granted to the federal government and those reserved to the states or to the people. All of us need to be reminded that the federal government did not create the states. The States created the federal government.

Inaugural Address, January 20, 1981

All of us should remember that the federal government is not some mysterious institution comprised of buildings, files, and paper. The people are the government. What we create we ought to be able to control.

The President's News Conference, January 29, 1981

I can't help thinking that, while much of the 20th Century saw the rise of the federal government, the 21st Century will be the century of the states. I have always believed that America is strongest and freest and happiest when it is truest to the wisdom of its founders.

Remarks to the annual meeting of the National Governors' Association, Cincinnati, Ohio, August 8, 1988

The explorers of the modern era are the entrepreneurs. Men with vision; with the courage to take risks, and faith enough to brave the unknown.

Remarks and a Question and Answer Session with the students and faculty at Moscow State University, May 31, 1988

And on my way to the hall, a fellow recognized me and asked me what I was doing in Las Vegas. And I told him what I was there for. And he said 'What are a bunch of farmers doing in a place like Las Vegas?' And I couldn't resist. I said, 'Buster, they're in a business that makes a Las Vegas crap table look like a guaranteed annual income.'

Remarks to State Officers of the Future Farmers of America, July 29, 1987

Our young friends—yes, young friends, for in our hearts you will always be young, full of the love that is youth, love of life, love of joy, love of country—you fought for your country and for its safety and for the freedom of others with strength and courage. We love you for it. We honor you. And we have faith that as He does all His sacred children, the Lord will bless you and keep you, the Lord will make his face to shine upon you and give you peace, now and forevermore.

Remarks at the Veterans Day Ceremony at the Vietnam Veterans Memorial, November 11, 1988

In eight short years, we have reversed a 50-year trend of turning to the government for solutions. We have relearned what our Founding Fathers knew long ago—it is the people, not the government, who provide the vitality and creativity that make a great nation. Just as the first American Revolution, which began with the shot heard 'round the world, inspired people everywhere who dreamed of freedom, so has this second American revolution inspired changes throughout the world. The message that we brought to Washington—reduce government, reduce regulation, restore incentives—has been heard around the world. I leave this office secure in the knowledge that these policies have worked, and confident that this great Nation will continue to lead the way toward freedom and prosperity for all mankind.

Letter accompanying the Annual Economic Report of the President, January 10, 1989

54

Common sense told us that when you put a big tax on something, the people will produce less of it. So, we cut the people's tax rates, and the people produced more than ever before.

Farewell Address to the Nation, January 11, 1989

I hope my legacy will mean that we restore the balance between the levels of government, meaning that we restore to local and state government functions that are properly theirs and belong there, and restore to them the tax sources necessary to support them, which have been also usurped by the federal government; that we set a policy that I would hope could be legally imposed, barring an emergency such as war, that the federal government, like the various states, must live within its means. And a policy, before I leave, that we could begin, no matter how small, paying installments on the national debt as a signal to those who follow, that the national debt is not something that we will … hang over, forever, succeeding generations.

Interview with reporters from the Los Angeles Times, *January 20, 1982*

No government in the history of civilization has ever voluntarily reduced itself in size. But with God's help, this one's going to.

Remarks at the opening ceremonies for the Knoxville International Energy Exposition (World's Fair), Tennessee, May 1, 1982

During my lifetime, I have seen the rise of fascism and communism. Both philosophies glorify the arbitrary power of the state. These ideologies held, at first, a certain fascination for some intellectuals. But both theories fail. Both deny those God-given liberties that are the inalienable right of each person on this planet; indeed, they deny the existence of God. Because of this fundamental flaw, fascism has already been destroyed, and the bankruptcy of communism has been laid bare for all to see—a system that is efficient in producing machines of war but cannot feed its people.

I have not come to China to hold forth on what divides us, but to build on what binds us. I have not come to dwell on a closed-door past, but to urge that Americans and Chinese look to the future, because together we can, and we will, make tomorrow a better day.

Remarks to Chinese community leaders in Beijing, China, April 27, 1984

My goal is to keep America the premier job-creating nation on Earth, and we intend to unleash the full power of entrepreneurship. Together, we can seize this historic moment. We can create a new Tax Code—clean, simple, and fair. We can make ours the land of the future, offering unlimited opportunity to all Americans who dare to live for their dreams.

Radio Address to the Nation on Tax Reform, April 13, 1985

In the swirl of issues and events that is Washington, there remains one overriding purpose, the purpose toward which everything else we do in this town is—or should be—aimed. I guess I would define it this way: Creating a peaceful and safe world in which we can all securely enjoy the rights and the freedoms that have been given to us by God. Being free and prosperous in a world at peace.

That's our ultimate goal. That is, as you might say, the business at hand here in Washington.

Remarks at a White House briefing for Republican student interns on Soviet-United States Relations, July 29, 1986

Well, I believe that we have started government on a different course, different than anything we've done in the last half century since Roosevelt began with the New Deal. And that is the recognition that there must be a limit to government size and power; that there has been a distortion of the relationship between the various echelons of government—federal, state, and local.

Interview with reporters from the Los Angeles Times, *January 20, 1982*

58

The Council on Wage and Price Stability … has been a failure. It has been totally ineffective in controlling inflation …. Therefore, I am now ending the wage and price program of the Council.

(By 1984, inflation was cut from an annual rate of 12.4 percent to 3.2 percent.) Presidential News Conference, January 29, 1981

I was thinking on the way over here what a great idea this event is and wondering why we don't get together more often. You know, it kind of reminds me of the fellah who asked his friend what the problem really was: Ignorance or apathy. And the friend responded, "I don't know, and I don't care."

Remarks at a White House briefing on Foreign Policy, March 15, 1988

As we view changes which seem to be happening in the Soviet Union with cautious optimism, let it be remembered that, four decades ago, the Kremlin rejected Soviet participation in the Marshall plan. If the current Soviet leadership seeks another path, if they reject the closed, isolated, and belligerent policies they inherited, if they wish their country to be part of the free world economy, we welcome the change. Let there be no mistake: The Soviet government is subject to the same rules as any other. Any government which is part of our deals with the West's major economic institutions must do so with good faith, open books, and open government on which both depend. Economic transactions are not

maneuvers for political gain or international leverage; such destructive tactics are not tolerated. Countries which are part of the system are expected to do their best to strengthen the process and institutions or be condemned to economic isolation.

The Soviet Union must also understand that the price of entry into the community of prosperous and productive nations is not just an economic price. There is a political price of even greater significance: Respect for and support for the values of freedom that are, in the end, the true engines of material prosperity. Time will tell if the signs emanating from the Soviet Union reflect real change or illusion. The decisions made by the Soviet leaders themselves will determine if relations will bloom or wither. Any agreement to reduce nuclear weapons, for example, must be followed by reductions in conventional forces.

Remarks on signing the George C. Marshall Month Proclamation, June 1, 1987

The economic welfare of all our people must ultimately stem not from government programs, but from the wealth created by a vigorous private sector. What is more just than allowing individuals to benefit from their work and talent? Nothing is more unfair than the tax imposed by inflation, which hits those least able to protect themselves. Our policies reducing inflation and favoring growth are in fact the most efficient and the only sustainable way of achieving widespread economic opportunity and prosperity.

Statement to French newspaper, December 22, 1983

Where, I have at times asked myself, where do you all come from? How have you managed to cohere into the crack, disciplined, patriotic band of brothers I see before me this morning? Well, the answer's simple. You come from the southwest and the northeast, from the Rockies and the Adirondacks, from the inner cities and the most remote of farms. You come from America, and you are America's pride. And on behalf of all America, I thank you and pray God that He may bless you now and forever.

Remarks at the Armed Forces Farewell Salute in Camp Springs, Maryland, January 12, 1989

During my 1980 campaign for office, I called for a North American accord—a renewed spirit of friendship and cooperation between the United States, Mexico, and Canada, the three great nations which share this continent. I was delighted to see that spirit so much in evidence yesterday in Mexicali. And I'm confident that this spirit of friendship among our three countries will mark 1986 and the years beyond.

Radio Address to the Nation on Relations with Mexico and Canada, January 4, 1986

We have long since discovered that nothing lasts longer than a temporary government program.

Remarks at Herbert Hoover Library, West Branch, Iowa, August 8,1992

And on the Republican side, your support and guidance has been a valuable asset. I don't take it for granted. There's one thing—you can't be called a rubber stamp. I found that out on the tax bill. It's kind of like a happy marriage though. You have quarrels, and it's still a happy marriage.

Remarks at a Congressional barbecue on the South Lawn of The White House, September 30, 1982

You know, I told my senior staff in this room the other day that one definition of an economist is someone who sees something happen in practice and wonders if it would work in theory. That's one I can tell; my degree was in economics.

Remarks to business leaders during a White House briefing on Budget Reform, March 13, 1987

When the government takes away incentives to work and save, the economy goes flat—millions are thrown out of work and government revenues plunge.

Remarks to Congressional Leaders during a White House briefing on the Fiscal Year 1986 Budget, February 4, 1985

We didn't come to Washington for business as usual. We came here to rewrite the rulebook and to extend the boundaries of the possible. And, together with the American people, we've transformed economic decline and national pessimism into 37 months of economic growth and confidence. Productivity is up; 9 million new jobs have been created in just over three years. We've got a higher percentage of our citizens working today than have ever worked before in our history. In the past three years, real business fixed investment has risen ... a whopping 38 percent. And the stock market has climbed right through the roof.

Remarks at the 1986 Reagan Administration Executive Forum, February 6, 1986

I confess, I was not as attentive as I might have been during my classroom days. I seem to remember my parents being told, "Young Ron is trying—very trying."

Remarks at the annual convention of the National Parent-Teacher Association, Albuquerque, New Mexico, June 15, 1983

One of my favorite stories about government had to do with an employee who sat at a desk. And papers came to his desk; he read them and determined where they were to go and initialed them and sent them on. And one day a classified document came there. But it came to him, so he read it, and sent it on. Twenty-four hours later it came back to him with a note attached that said, "You weren't suppose to see this. Erase your initials, and initial the erasure."

Remarks on receiving the final report of the President's Private Sector Survey on Cost Control in the Federal Government, January 16, 1984

In closing, I know some of you are wondering if I'm going to say that line from the certain movie. But I know better than to take sides. So I've come up with what I hope will be a good compromise. As you may know, tomorrow I will flip the coin to officially start the game. So if you'll permit a little modification: Will you tell your teams to go out there and win one for the Flipper?

Remarks at a USC/Notre Dame Luncheon, Los Angeles, Califonia, November 23, 1990

Today, free enterprise is propelling us into a new technological era. Small businesses throughout our land now have computer capability, which a decade ago was available only to large corporations. The economic vitality pushing our country into the 21st Century is broad-based and irreversible. It's not coming from the top, but from the bottom. The creative talents of our citizenry, always America's greatest asset, are being magnified by state-of-the-art technology and put to work for our benefit as never before. We have every reason to be optimistic.

Remarks at the annual Conservative Political Action Conference Luncheon, February 20, 1987

A foreign policy based on our bedrock principles allows us to offer a practical solution to the suffering peoples of the world, a means of achieving prosperity and political stability that all Americans take for granted as their birthright.

Remarks to the American Enterprise Institute for Public Policy Research, December 7, 1988

61

You see, at first, when someone says, "Let's impose tariffs on foreign imports," it looks like they're doing the patriotic thing by protecting American products and jobs. And sometimes for a short while it works—but only for a short time. What eventually occurs is: First, homegrown industries start relying on government protection in the form of high tariffs. They stop competing and stop making innovative management and technological changes they need to succeed in world markets. And then while this is going on, something even worse occurs. High tariffs inevitably lead to retaliation by foreign countries and the triggering of fierce trade wars.

Radio Address to the Nation on Free and Fair Trade, April 25, 1987

Back then [before 1981], government's view of the economy could be summed up in a few short phrases: If it moves, tax it. If it keeps moving, regulate it. And if it stops moving, subsidize it.

Remarks to State Chairpersons of the National White House Conference on Small Business, August 15, 1986

I've always thought that the common sense and wisdom of government were summed up in a sign they used to have hanging on that gigantic Hoover Dam. It said, "Government property. Do not remove."

Remarks at the annual meeting of the National Alliance of Business, September 14, 1987

The willingness of our citizens to give freely and unselfishly of themselves, even their lives, in defense of our democratic principles, gives this great Nation continued strength and vitality. From Valley Forge to Vietnam, through war and peace, valiant Americans have answered the call to duty with honor and dignity.

Americans throughout this great land set aside Veterans Day for special remembrance of the men and women who have served to protect our freedom. The sound of bugles playing taps will pierce the air at countless ceremonies around the country and at our bases overseas in tribute to those who give their lives in order to safeguard human liberty.

Proclamation for Veterans Day, October 26, 1981

To protect our prosperity, the President needs the line-item veto, and America needs a constitutionally-mandated balanced budget.

Remarks at the annual Republican Congressional Fundraising Dinner, May 11, 1988

I've learned in Washington, that that's the only place where sound travels faster than light.

Remarks at the annual convention of the Congressional Medal of Honor Society in New York, New York, December 12, 1983

When the Constitution was written, it took longer to travel from Washington to Richmond, Virginia, than it does today to travel from Washington to Tokyo. The needs of the new world economy are transcending political boundaries.

Remarks and a Question and Answer Session with Members of the City Club of Cleveland, Ohio, January 11, 1988

The best view of big government is in the rearview mirror as we leave it behind.

Spirit of America Rally, Atlanta, Georgia, January 26, 1984

62

I should warn you that things in this city aren't often the way they seem. Where but in Washington would they call the department that's in charge of everything outdoors, everything outside, the Department of the Interior.

Remarks at the Fundraising Dinner of the Republican National Hispanic Assembly, September 14, 1983

The values and the valor of those Continental soldiers helped to release the freedom this blessed nation now enjoys. The vigilance and training of today's soldiers keep that freedom secure. Yes, meeting the defense budget calls for sacrificing other ways we might like to spend those funds. But this is a small sacrifice compared to that of America's colonial citizens. They paid with their blood and long years of hardship.

Remarks following investiture as an Honorary Member of the Society of the Cincinnati, February 21, 1983

America's open market is its great strength, not its weakness. International trade has helped bring unparalleled prosperity to the American people. It would be a tragic mistake to surrender to doubt and defeatism just when our prospects are looking so bright. I have confidence in America, and I'm sure you do too.

Radio Address to the Nation on International Trade, March 12, 1988

63

In just a few hours I'll undertake one of the saddest journeys of my Presidency. I'll be going to Andrews Air Force Base to meet one of our Air Force planes bringing home sixteen Americans who died this week in the terrorist attack on the United States Embassy in Beirut.

I undertake this task in great sadness, but also with a tremendous sense of pride in those who sacrificed their lives in our country's efforts to bring peace to the Middle East and spare others the agony of war. Greater love hath no man. The courage and dedication of these men and women reflect the best tradition of our Foreign Service, our Armed Forces, and the other departments and agencies whose personnel serve our nation overseas, often in situations of great personal danger.

Radio Address to the Nation on the Death of Federal Diplomatic and Military Personnel in Beirut, Lebanon, April 23, 1983

It is, in a way, an odd thing to honor those who died in defense of our country, in defense of us, in wars far away. The imagination plays a trick. We see these soldiers in our mind as old and wise. We see them as something like the Founding Fathers, grave and gray haired. But most of them were boys when they died, and they gave up two lives— the one they were living and the one they would have lived. When they died, they gave up their chance to be husbands and fathers and grandfathers. They gave up their chance to be revered old men. They gave up everything for our country, for us. And all we can do is remember.

Remarks at the Veterans Day Wreath-Laying Ceremony at Arlington National Cemetery, November 11, 1985

NATO will soon begin its fifth decade. The North Atlantic alliance is the most successful in history. While other alliances have been formed to win wars, our fundamental purpose is to prevent war while preserving and extending the frontiers of freedom.

Remarks to reporters following the North Atlantic Treaty Organization Summit Meeting in Brussels, Belgium, March 3, 1988

In closing, let me say that nothing made me prouder as President than America's young people in uniform. And no decision was ever more difficult for me to make than the times I ordered our military forces into action. Each time I issued an order, I reminded myself that it wasn't just a nameless, faceless soldier I was dispatching, but a child of loving parents, the partner of an adoring spouse or perhaps the parent and provider for some happy children. I reminded myself that if things should go wrong, and casualties did occur, it wouldn't just be a day of flag-draped coffins coming home.

There would permanently be empty chairs at family tables, vacant seats in Little League bleachers, and teary-eyed explanations to young children about why their daddy wouldn't be coming home again.

So I felt then, as I feel now, America owes a special thanks to those who are willing to make the ultimate sacrifice for their country. We must honor them and respect them, not just when they are in battle, but every day they wear the proud uniform of our country.

Commencement Address, The Citadel, May 15, 1993

65

Recently, one of our young … Marine lieutenant[s] flying a Cobra was in Grenada, and then went on to Beirut. And from there, he wrote back to the Armed Forces Journal something that he had been doing. He said that he noticed that every news story about the Grenada rescue mission contained a line—every story—that Grenada produces more nutmeg than any other place in the world. And he decided that was a code, and he was going to break the code. And he did.

He wrote back and said: "Number one: Grenada produces more nutmeg than any place in the world. Number two: The Soviets and the Cubans are trying to take Grenada. Number three: You can't make good eggnog without nutmeg. And, number four: You can't have Christmas without eggnog. Number five: The Soviets and the Cubans are trying to steal Christmas. And, number six: We stopped them."

Remarks to the Reagan Administration Executive Forum, January 20, 1984

When our Founding Fathers designed this government—of, by, and for the people—they never imagined what we've come to know as the progressive income tax. When the income tax was first levied in 1913, the top rate was only 7 percent on people with incomes over $500,000. Now, that's the equivalent of multimillionaires today. But in our lifetime we've seen marginal tax rates skyrocket as high as 90 percent, and not even the poor have been spared … . I'm certain that the bill I'm signing today is not only an historic overhaul of our tax code and a sweeping victory for fairness, it's also the best anti-poverty bill, the best pro-family, and the best job-creation program ever to come out of the Congress of the United States.

Remarks on signing the Tax Reform Act of 1986, October 22, 1986

In James Michener's book, *The Bridges at Toko-Ri,* he writes of an officer waiting through the night for the return of planes to a carrier as dawn is coming on. And he asks, "Where do we find such men?" Well, we find them where we've always found them. They are the product of the freest society man has ever known. They make a commitment to the military—make it freely, because the birthright we share as Americans is worth defending.

Radio Address on National Armed Forces Day, May 15, 1982

In the Middle East, in particular, a strong, credible America remains the best guarantor of Israel's integrity and survival as a free nation. A strong, credible America is also an indispensable incentive for a peaceful resolution of differences between Israel and her neighbors. America has never flinched from its commitment to the State of Israel—a commitment which remains unshakable.

Remarks to the National Conference of Christians and Jews, New York, New York, March 23, 1982

England may be the mother of parliaments, but from the Boston Tea Party to this administration, it's the United States that has been the mother of tax revolts. You know, that's a pretty good line. I can hardly wait to try it out on Margaret Thatcher.

Remarks at a White House briefing for members of the American Business Conference, March 23, 1988

The American taxing structure, the purpose of which was to serve the people, began instead to serve the insatiable appetite of government. If you will forgive me, you know someone has likened government to a baby. It is an alimentary canal with an appetite at one end and no sense of responsibility at the other.

Remarks before a Joint Session of the Canadian Parliament, Ottawa, March 11, 1981

Well, Teddy Roosevelt reminded us long ago that the cry of the weakling counts for little in the move toward peace, but the call of a just man armed is potent. Well, to put Teddy in modern terms: Speak softly, but keep the battleship Iowa close at hand.

Remarks to the annual Leadership Conference of the American Legion, February 10, 1987

With Americans in the lead, entrepreneurs have created a global electronic network, on-line 24 hours a day, sending capital, ideas, goods and services around the world at near the speed of light.

Remarks at a Question and Answer Session with members of the City Club of Cleveland, Ohio, January 11, 1988

We're not merely accelerating the processes of the Industrial Revolution; we're fundamentally transforming it. Let me give you just one example: The semiconductor, or computer chip. One scientist makes this comparison: If automotive technology had progressed as fast as semiconductor technology in the past 20 years, he says, a Rolls Royce would now cost less than $3, get 3 million miles to the gallon, deliver enough power to drive an ocean liner, and six of them would fit on the head of a pin.

Remarks and a Question and Answer Session with members of the City Club of Cleveland, Ohio, January 11, 1988

F.D.R. also expressed his belief in giving back to the states authorities which he said had been unjustly usurped by the federal government. And I figure if we give enough of them back, then I'm going to be able to go to the ranch more often.

Toast at a White House Dinner honoring the Nation's Governors, February 23, 1982

Tragic turmoil in the Middle East runs back to the dawn of history. In our modern day, conflict after conflict has taken its brutal toll there. In an age of nuclear challenge and economic interdependence, such conflicts are a threat to all the people of the Middle East itself. It's time for us all— in the Middle East and around the world—to call a halt to conflict, hatred and prejudice. It's time for us all to launch a common effort for reconstruction, peace, and progress.

Address to the Nation on United States Policy for Peace in the Middle East, September 1, 1982

There are some who seem to believe that we should run up the American flag in defense of our markets. They would embrace protectionism again and insulate our markets from world competition. Well, the last time the United States tried that, there was enormous economic distress in the world. World trade fell by 60 percent, and young Americans soon followed the American flag into World War II.

I'm old enough and, hopefully, wise enough not to forget the lesson of those unhappy years. The world must never live through such a nightmare again. We're in the same boat with our trading partners. If one partner shoots a hole in the boat, does it make sense for the other one to shoot another hole in the boat? Some say yes, and call it getting tough. Well, I call it stupid. We shouldn't be shooting holes; we should be working together to plug them up. We must strengthen the boat of free markets and fair trade so it can lead the world to economic recovery and greater political stability.

Radio Address to the Nation on International Free Trade, November 20, 1982

69

You know I've never been very good, myself, at fundraising. And I've told some of my friends on occasion … That's why I got in government, because we don't ask for it, we just take it.

Remarks at the Awards Presentation Ceremony for the President's Committee on the Arts and the Humanities, May 17, 1983

My friends, history is clear: Lower tax rates mean greater freedom, and whenever we lower the tax rates, our entire nation is better off.

Remarks to business leaders in Cincinnati, Ohio, October 3, 1985

When our administration came to office, we took it as one of our chief aims to reawaken the federalist impulse and approach the Constitution with a new fidelity— in short, to restore the power to the states.

Remarks to the National Conference of State Legislators, January 29, 1988

I just wanted to speak to you about something from the Internal Revenue Code. It is the last sentence of section 509A of the code and it reads: "For purposes of paragraph 3, an organization described in paragraph 2 shall be deemed to include an organization described in section 501C-4, 5, or 6, which would be described in paragraph 2 if it were an organization described in section 501C-3." And that's just one sentence out of those 57 feet of books.

Remarks to the Dothan-Houston County Chamber of Commerce in Dothan, Alabama, July 10, 1986

You know, the difference between local government and Washington is very simple. Recently, there was a little town. Their traffic signs were only five feet high, and they decided to raise them, for better visibility for the motorists, to raise them seven feet above the ground. And the federal government came in and said that they had a program that would do that for them. They lowered the pavement two feet.

Remarks at a Target '82 Republican Fundraising Reception in Los Angeles, California, August 17, 1981

"To see the universe in a grain of sand" is no longer a poetic metaphor, but the daily reality of the silicon chip. F. Scott Fitzgerald wrote that when the early explorers first looked on this land, they must have held their breath. They had, for the last time in history, come face-to-face with something commensurate to man's infinite capacity for wonder. Yet it was not the last time. We, too, stand on the shores of something as vast—of an economic and technological future immense with promise.

Remarks at the annual meeting of the Atlantic Council, June 13, 1988

Now, diplomacy, of course, is a subtle and nuanced craft, so much so that it's said that when one of the most wily diplomats of the 19th Century passed away, other diplomats asked, on reports of his death, "What do you suppose the old fox meant by that?"

Address to the 42nd Session of the United Nations General Assembly, New York, New York, September 21, 1987

In a quiet but final way, the course of human events was forever altered when, on a ridge overlooking the Emmitsburg Pike in an obscure Pennsylvania town called Gettysburg, Lincoln spoke of our duty to government of and by the people and never letting it perish from the earth. At the start of this decade, I suggested that we live in equally momentous times, that it is up to us now to decide whether our form of government would endure and whether history still had a place of greatness for a quiet, pleasant, greening land called America. Not everything has been made perfect in seven years, nor will it be made perfect in seven times 70 years, but before us, this year and beyond, are great prospects for the cause of peace and world freedom.

Address before a Joint Session of Congress on the State of the Union, January 25, 1988

Fortunately, we and our allies have rediscovered the strength of our common democratic values, and we're applying them as a cornerstone of a comprehensive strategy for peace with freedom. In London last year, I announced the commitment of the United States to developing the infrastructure of democracy throughout the world. We intend to pursue this democratic initiative vigorously. The future belongs not to governments and ideologies which oppress their peoples, but to democratic systems of self-government which encourage individual initiative and guarantee personal freedom.

Address before a Joint Session of Congress on the State of the Union, January 25, 1983

71

When John F. Kennedy's tax program that he recommended and which was not too dissimilar to ours, when it was passed, the same thing happened—more revenues at lower rates. It happened back in Coolidge's administration, and they cut the taxes several times in that period. I can show you again where tax increases have resulted in lower revenues for the government because of the harmful effect they have on the economy by reducing incentive and so forth.

Remarks and a Question and Answer Session with economic reporters, June 16, 1987

You know, thinking about what your group has been through reminds me of the story of the three gentlemen who had departed this earth and where standing at the gates of heaven waiting for admittance. One was a surgeon, the other one an engineer, the third one an economist. They'd all been good, upright people, but it developed that there was only room inside for one. So St. Peter said, "I'll tell you what, I'll pick the one who comes from the oldest profession." The surgeon stepped right up, and he said, "Well, I'm your man. Right

after God created Adam, he operated. He took a rib, created Eve, so surgery has to be the oldest profession." And the engineer said, "No." He said, "You see, before God created Adam and Eve, he took the chaos that prevailed and built the earth in six days. So, engineering had to precede surgery." The economist spoke up and said, "Just a minute. Who do you think created all that chaos?"

Remarks at the annual convention of the United States League of Savings Associations, New Orleans, Louisiana, November 16, 1982

I'm afraid that I have to confess to you that one of the sins of government, and one with which we must deal and never be able to be completely successful with, and this includes our own government, is that the bureaucracy once created has one fundamental rule above all others: Preserve the bureaucracy.

The President's News Conference following the Soviet-United States Summit Meeting in Moscow, USSR, June 1, 1988

I can't go without just telling another little thing—maybe it's a little unkind of me—about government, but what planted some of these thoughts in my mind a long time ago—I was in the military. And I remember a case arose in World War II for a warehouse that was full of filing cabinets, and the filing cabinets were all full of papers. But research revealed that none of these records were of any value whatsoever or served any purpose in the government. They were outmoded papers and so forth. They had no historical value. And so, up through the channels went a request to destroy these papers and empty the filing cabinets so they could be used now for the great need—or then, at that time—of the papers that were current and so forth. And back down through the channels from the top came the answer to that request: Permission granted to destroy all of these records, provided copies were made of each one.

Remarks to representatives of the Future Farmers of America, July 28, 1988

Welcome here to your house, which you're letting me live in for a while.

*Remarks at a White House reception opening the
"Champions of American Sport" Exhibition,
June 22, 1981*

Some of my hard-working aides recommended against leaving the Capital and coming all the way out here. So to keep them happy, I decided. I said, "Okay, we'll flip a coin to decide whether to visit your beautiful State or stay in Washington." And you know something? I had to flip 14 times before it came out right. So, then I got them all together, and I said, "Boys, we're going where the people think big and the sky's the limit." You know what I meant; they didn't. They all headed for Tip O'Neill's office.

Remarks at a Republican Party Rally in Great Falls, Montana, October 28, 1982

I'll tell the story of a friend of mine who was asked to a costume ball a short time ago. He slapped some egg on his face and went as a liberal economist.

Appointment of a member of the President's Commission on White House Fellowships, February 11, 1988

You know, I can confess to this group that I've been accused of being pro-business. Well, I just have to say: Guilty as charged.

Remarks at a White House briefing for minority business owners, July 15, 1987

In dealing with our economy, more is in question than just prosperity. Ultimately, peace and freedom are at stake. The United States took the lead after World War II in creating an international trading and financial system that limited government's ability to disrupt trade. We did this because history had taught us the freer the flow of trade across the borders, the greater the world economic progress and the greater the impetus for world peace.

Remarks to the Commonwealth Club of California, San Francisco, March 4, 1983

When the liberals say "family," they mean "Big Brother in Washington." When we say "family," we mean "honor thy father and mother."

Remarks at a Republican Party Rally in Waco, Texas, September 22, 1988

One of the most dangerous inclinations of human nature, Thomas Jefferson once said, is appropriating wealth produced by the labors of others rather than producing it with one's own labor. He said government was the usual vehicle for this abuse. And as he put it: The stronger the government, the weaker the producer. And he added: The natural progress of things is for liberty to yield and government to gain ground.

Remarks to Broan Manufacturing Company employees in Hartford, Wisconsin, July 27, 1987

I thought it was extraordinary that Richard Nixon went on *Meet the Press* and spent an entire hour with Chris Wallace, Tom Brokaw, and John Chancellor. That should put an end to that talk that he's been punished enough.

Remarks at the annual White House Correspondents Association Dinner, April 21, 1988

Well, before we came into office, many entrepreneurs thought federal regulators and paperwork would never go away. But we've ripped 40,000 pages from the federal book of regulations. We've eliminated what seems to be about 600 million man hours a year of filling out government paperwork. We came into office with a strategy: Lower tax rates, less regulation, monetary stability, and controlling federal spending through a constitutional amendment to balance the budget. Now, we put three of these four parts into practice, together with reducing the rate of growth in federal spending, and you know the results: Four of the best years in history.

Remarks at the National Federation of Independent Business Conference, June 23, 1987

I've always believed that a lot of the troubles in the world would disappear if we were talking to each other instead of about each other.

Remarks at Ford Claycomo Assembly Plant, Kansas City, Missouri, April 11, 1984

Twice in my lifetime, I have seen the peoples of Europe plunged into the tragedy of war. Twice in my lifetime, Europe has suffered destruction and military occupation in wars that statesmen proved powerless to prevent, soldiers unable to contain, and ordinary citizens unable to escape. And twice in my lifetime, young Americans have bled their lives into the soil of those battlefields not to enrich our domain, but to restore the peace and independence of our friends and allies.

All of us who lived through those troubled times share a common resolve that they must never come again. And most of us share a common appreciation of the Atlantic Alliance that has made a peaceful, free, and prosperous Western Europe in the post-war era possible.

Remarks to members of the National Press Club on Arms Reduction and Nuclear Weapons, November 18, 1981

Permit me to tell you what those of us in government intend to do as our part of this quest for excellence. And by the way, you can relax: I know that others have given you thorough briefings, so I promise to keep my own remarks short. You know, I often reflect that George Washington—I try to keep this in mind—gave an inaugural address of just 135 words and became, of course, a great President. And then there was William Henry Harrison. Harrison gave an inaugural address that droned on for nearly two hours. It was a blustery March day. Harrison caught pneumonia, and a month later he was dead.

75

Remarks at the annual Conservative Political Action Conference Luncheon, February 20, 1987

It is old-fashioned, even reactionary to remind people that free enterprise has done more to reduce poverty than all the government programs dreamed up by democrats.

Address as Governor of California, 1972

Maintenance of our allied partnerships is a key to our foreign policy. The bedrock of European security remains the NATO alliance. NATO is not just a military alliance; it's a voluntary political community of free men and women based on shared principles and a common history. The ties that bind us to our European allies are not the brittle ties of expediency or the weighty shackles of compulsion. They resemble what Abraham Lincoln called the "mystic chords of memory," uniting peoples who share a common vision. So, let there be no doubt on either side of the Atlantic: The freedom and independence of America's allies remain as dear to us as our own.

Remarks at the annual Washington Conference of the American Legion, February 22, 1983

Two centuries ago, in a hall much smaller than this one, in Philadelphia, Americans met to draft a Constitution. In the course of their debates, one of them said that the new government, if it was to rise high, must be built on the broadest base: The will and the consent of the people. And so it was, and so it has been.

My message today is that the dreams of ordinary people reach to astonishing heights. If we diplomatic pilgrims are to achieve equal altitudes, we must build all we do on the full breadth of humanity's will and consent and the full expanse of the human heart.

Address to the 42nd Session of the United Nations General Assembly, New York, New York, September 21, 1987

When it comes to the economy, there are two big facts to keep in mind. Before we came to Washington, our economy was in a mess: Inflation in double digits, men and women being thrown out of jobs, the prime interest rate soaring at the highest level since the Civil War. And the second big fact—well, the second big fact is that when our administration had put its economic program in place, the economy stopped shrinking and started to grow, and it's been growing ever since.

Radio Address to the Nation on the Economy, July 16, 1988

I think it's time for new ideas that can produce real solutions. And the best social program is a productive job for anyone who's willing to work. That's why we're urging the private sector to get more actively involved in job training and urban development. The business of business is America. And that's why we're calling on the Congress to take prompt action on our enterprise free zone proposal. I am inspired to press for that after what I've seen that has happened here without our enterprise proposal.

Remarks at a luncheon with local elected officials and businessmen, Baltimore, Maryland, July 13, 1982

I have a dream that some day we can provide you with the revenue sources that have been co-opted by the federal government, so that local money no longer has to make a round trip through Washington before you can use it back in your local area—minus a certain carrying charge.

Remarks at the annual meeting of the National Association of Towns and Townships, September 12, 1983

Seventy-seven years after it was adopted, Lord Acton said of the men who had written the Constitution that "they had solved with astonishing and unexampled success two problems which had hitherto baffled the capacity of the most enlightened nations: They had contrived a system of federal government which … increased the national power, and yet respected local liberties and authorities. They had founded it on the principle of equality, without surrendering the securities for property and freedom." Well, here, for the first time in the history of the world was a system in which man would not be beholden to government; government would be beholden to man.

The explicit promise in the Declaration that we're endowed by our Creator with certain inalienable rights was meant for all of us. It wasn't meant to be limited or perverted by special privilege or by double standards that favor one group over another. It is a principle for eternity, America's deepest treasure.

Remarks at the annual meeting of the American Bar Association, Atlanta, Georgia, August 1, 1983

You younger people: I grew up in the era of the Depression, and there are others in the room who did also. Anyone who tells you that we don't have compassion for someone who's lost his job doesn't know what they're talking about, because we saw that great tragedy.

We all wish there were some quick and easy cure for this terrible economic illness that was so long in the making. For months now, I've been biting my tongue while I've listened to all those strident speeches about how we've purposely thrown people out of work. Well it seems to me that the people who have created the mess we're in, the same politicians who took us down the path of guaranteed economic disaster, are the last ones who should be delivering sermons on the cause of unemployment.

Remarks at a Virginia Republican Party Rally, Richmond, Virginia, September 29, 1982

Status quo, you know, that is Latin for "the mess we're in."

Remarks at a reception for members of the Associated General Contractors of America, March 16, 1981

We've gone astray from first principles. We've lost sight of the rule that individual freedom and ingenuity are at the very core of everything that we've accomplished. Government's first duty is to protect the people, not run their lives.

Remarks at the National Conference of the Building and Construction Trades, AFL-CIO, March 30, 1981

There is nothing wrong with our system. Somebody is handling the machinery wrong.

Interview as Governor of California, 1973

Somebody told me—this is another news announcement—that Dave Stockman is getting married. His toughest budget battles lie ahead.

Remarks at a Congressional barbecue on the South Lawn of The White House, September 30, 1982

Let us cut through the fog for a moment. The answer to a government that's too big is to stop feeding its growth.

Address before a Joint Session of Congress on the Program for Economic Recovery, April 28, 1981

Somebody did quite a research job, though, to find a picture of me in the Dixon YMCA band. This should lay to rest the rumor that photography had yet to be invented when I was that age.

Remarks at the annual Foundation Luncheon of the YMCA of Metropolitan Chicago, Illinois, May 10, 1982

At home, our enemy is no longer Red Coats but red ink.

Remarks on signing a proclamation commemorating the 200th Anniversary of the British Surrender at Yorktown, September 14, 1981

We've long thought there were two things in Washington that are unbalanced—the budget and the liberals.

Remarks at the annual dinner of the Conservative Political Action Conference, March 1, 1985

What we're trying to do is alter the economic situation in our country by changing one simple two-letter word, economic control by government to economic control on government.

Toasts at a dinner honoring the Nation's Governors, February 24, 1981

As some of you know, we've had our headaches lately. The big spenders in the Congress are at it again—present company not included in those. They've been inventing their miracle cures for which there are no known diseases.

Remarks to members of Ohio Veterans Organizations, Columbus, Ohio, October 4, 1982

No one has yet found a way to repeal the law of supply and demand.

Address as Governor of California, 1972

79

Prosperity is something created by people and their industries and business for which government takes credit.

Address as Governor of California, 1973

Now, it's that simple. Our opponents want more money from your family budgets so they can spend it on the federal budget and make it remain high. Maybe it's time that you and millions like you remind them of a few simple facts. It's your money, not theirs. You earned it. They didn't. You have every right to keep a bigger share than you've been allowed to keep for a great many years now. When they insist we can't reduce taxes and spending and balance the budget too, one six-word answer will do: "Yes, we can. And yes, we will."

For too long, government has stood in the way of taking more of what our people earn, no matter how hard they try. It's almost become economics without a soul. And that's why the ultimate goal in everything that we're trying to do is to give this economy back to the American people.

Remarks on the Program for Economic Recovery at a White House reception for business and government leaders, June 11, 1981

When you start talking about government as "we" instead of "they", you have been in office too long.

Interview as Governor of California, 1973

The weakness in this country for too many years has been our insistence on leaving or carving an ever-increasing number of slices from a shrinking economic pie. Our policies have concentrated on rationing scarcity rather than creating plenty. As a result, our economy has stagnated. But those days are ending.

We must lift where we stand, struggle for tomorrow, and earn anew the reputation this country once had as the land of golden opportunity.

Remarks at the annual convention of the National League of Cities in Los Angeles, California, November 29, 1982

Too often, entrepreneurs are forgotten heroes. We rarely hear about them. But look into the heart of America, and you'll see them. They're the owners of that store down the street, the faithful who support our churches, schools, and communities, the brave people everywhere who produce our goods, feed a hungry world, and keep our homes and families warm while they invest in the future to build a better America.

Radio Address to the Nation on Small Business, May 14, 1983

Let's be clear about where the deficit problem comes from. Contrary to the drumbeat we've been hearing for the last few months, the deficits we face are not rooted in defense spending. Taken as a percentage of the gross national product, our defense spending happens to be only about four-fifths of what it was in 1970. Nor is the deficit, as some would have it, rooted in tax cuts. Even with our tax cuts, taxes as a fraction of gross national product remain about the same as they were in 1970. The fact is, our deficits come from the uncontrolled growth of the budget for domestic spending.

Address before a Joint Session of Congress on the State of the Union, January 25, 1983

Now, it's also time for some plain talk about the most immediate obstacle to controlling federal deficits. The simple but frustrating problem of making expenses match revenues—something American families do and the federal government can't—has caused crisis after crisis in this city. Mr Speaker, Mr. President, I will say to you tonight what I have said before and will continue to say: The budget process

has broken down; it needs a drastic overhaul. With each ensuing year, the spectacle before the American people is the same as it was this Christmas: Budget deadlines delayed or missed completely, monstrous continuing resolutions that pack hundreds of billions of dollars worth of spending into one bill, and a federal government on the brink of default.

Address before a Joint Session of Congress on the State of the Union, January 25, 1988

Our nation has forgotten or just overlooked the fact that government—any government—has a built-in tendency to grow.

We invented the assembly line and mass production, but punitive tax policies and excessive and unnecessary regulations plus government borrowing have stifled our ability to update plants and equipment.

Excessive taxation of individuals has robbed us of incentive.

Address to the Nation on the Economy, February 5, 1981

81

There's an old story about a farmer and a lawyer that illustrates my point:

It seems these two got into a pretty bad collision, a traffic accident. They both got out of their cars. The farmer took one look at the lawyer, walked back to his car, got a package, brought it back. There was a bottle inside, and he said, "Here, you look pretty shook up. I think you ought to take nip of this, it'll steady your nerves." Well, the lawyer did. And the farmer said, "You still look a little bit pale. How about another?" And the lawyer took another swallow. At the urging of the farmer, he took another and another and another. And then finally, he said he was feeling pretty good and asked the farmer if he didn't think that he ought to have a little nip, too. And the farmer said, "Not me, I'm waiting for the state Trooper."

Remarks at the annual Conservative Political Action Conference Dinner, February 18, 1983

82

Yes, the deficit doctors have their scalpels out all right, but they're not poised over the budget. That's as fat as ever and getting fatter. What they're ready to operate on is your wallet.

Remarks at a meeting of the National Association of Home Builders, May 16, 1983

There's been some criticism, however, that we don't have a definite foreign policy, that we haven't been doing enough about that, and that's not true at all. Just the other day, before he left for China, Al Haig sent a message to Brezhnev that said, "Roses are red, violets are blue, stay out of El Salvador and Poland, too."

Remarks at a White House reception for the Republican National Committee, June 12, 1981

Now, as most of you know, I'm not one for looking back. I figure there will be plenty of time for that when I get old!

Remarks at the Republican National Committee's 1994 Gala on the occasion of Ronald Reagan's 83rd Birthday, Washington D.C., February 3, 1994

Theodore Roosevelt was right when he said, "It is our duty to see that the wage worker, the small producer, the ordinary consumer, get their fair share of the benefit of business prosperity. But, it either is or ought to be evident to everyone, that business has to prosper before anybody can get any benefit from it."

Well, generation after generation of hard-working Americans have understood that truth and used it to build the most prosperous nation on earth. As I sign this report today, let us remember that success for small business and for America is one and the same.

I call on the Congress to work with us to hold down spending and protect the people's tax cuts. Let us remember that prosperity, like profits, must be earned. It'll never come as a gift from government or anyone else. If we return incentives to risk-takers and entrepreneurs, we'll free our people to create good times ahead, restoring hope and opportunity for everyone.

Remarks on signing the Annual Report on the State of Small Business, March 18, 1983

Tax rates are prices—prices for working, saving, and investing. And when you raise the price of those productive activities, you get less of them and more activity in the underground economy, tax shelters and leisure pursuits. You in small business understand that you can't force people to buy merchandise that isn't selling by raising your price. But too many in Washington and across the country still believe that we can raise more revenue from the economy by making it more expensive to work, save, and invest in the economy. We can't repeal human nature.

Remarks at the National Conference of the National Federation of Independent Business, June 22, 1983

I've been told that some members of Congress disagree with my tax cut proposal. Well, you know it's been said that taxation is the art of plucking the feathers without killing the bird. It's time they realized the bird just doesn't have any feathers left.

Remarks at the Mid-Winter Congressional City Conference of the National League of Cities, March 2, 1981

But we cannot compare labor-management relations in the private sector with government. Government cannot close down the assembly line. It has to provide without interruption the protective services which are government's reason for being.

It was in recognition of this that the Congress passed a law forbidding strikes by government employees against the public safety. Let me read the solemn oath taken by each of these employees, a sworn affidavit, when they accepted their jobs: "I am not participating in any strike against the Government of the United States or any agency thereof, and I will not so participate while an employee of the Government of the United States or any agency thereof."

It is for this reason that I must tell those who fail to report for duty this morning that they are in violation of the law, and if they do not report for work within 48 hours, they have forfeited their jobs and will be terminated.

Remarks and a Question and Answer Session with reporters on the Air Traffic Controllers Strike, August 3, 1981

But on the level, though, I like photographers. You don't ask questions. Can you imagine Sam Donaldson [ABC News] with a camera? As most of you would say, "The thought makes me shutter." Somebody asked me one day why we didn't put a stop to Sam's shouting out questions at us when we're out on the South Lawn. We can't. If we did, the starling would come back.

Remarks at the annual Awards Dinner of the White House News Photographers Association, May 18, 1983

Some believe that government planning is more efficient, so they rely on tax breaks and other subsidies to those businesses that already exist. But that never works.... [T]he most fertile and rapidly growing sector of any economy is that part that exists right now only as a dream in someone's head or an inspiration in his heart. No one can ever predict where the change will come from or foresee the industries of the future.

Address to Western Europe from the Venice Economic Summit, June 5, 1987

83

When I was in fifth grade, I'm not sure that I knew what a national debt was. Of course, when I was in the fifth grade, we didn't have one.

Remarks at a White House luncheon for members of the President's Advisory Council on Private Sector Initiatives, June 28, 1983

When government sets out to solve a problem, the cure may not be worse than the disease. But it is bigger and it costs more. Government does not really solve problems; it subsidizes them. And it does not produce a dime of revenue. It can spend only what it first takes from the pockets of the working men and women of this country.

Remarks at the American Textile Manufacturers Institute, San Francisco, California, March 29, 1973

Let's take the Job Corps. It's estimated that each job created through the program costs the taxpayers $15,200. That's almost equal to sending a student to Harvard for one year. Maybe the result's the same, too.

Remarks at a White House meeting with the Deficit Reduction Coalition, April 16, 1985

Two centuries ago in this country, small business owners—the merchants, the builders, the traders—rebelled against excessive taxation and government interference and helped found this nation. Today we are working to bring about another revolution, this time against the intolerable burdens inflation, over-regulation, and over-taxation have placed upon the nation's 12 million small businesses, which provide the livelihood for more than 100 million of our people.

To revitalize the nation, we must stimulate small business growth and opportunity. Small business accounts for over 60 percent of our jobs, half our business output, and at least half of the innovations that keep American industry strong.

Proclamation for Small Business Week, March 23, 1981

You see, we can either have an economy that puts the private citizen at the center—the consumer, the worker, the entrepreneur—and lets each individual be the judge of what to buy or sell, where to work, where to invest, and what to create. Or we can put the government at the center of the economy and let the bureaucrats and politicians call the balls and strikes and decide who's out of business, or who will get the big contract and be home free.

What is euphemistically called government-corporate partnership is just government coercion, political favoritism, collectivist industrial policy, and old-fashioned federal boondoggles nicely wrapped up in a bright colored ribbon. And it doesn't work. This kind of approach was tried in Europe, and it's being abandoned, because it only resulted in economic stagnation and industrial decay.

Remarks at a luncheon for Representative Connie Mack, Miami, Florida, June 29, 1988

I believe we really can, however, say that God did give mankind virtually unlimited gifts to invent, produce and create. And for that reason alone, it would be wrong for governments to devise a tax structure or economic system that suppresses and denies those gifts.

Remarks at a dinner honoring Representative Jack F. Kemp of New York, December 1, 1988

When a business or an individual spends more than it makes, it goes bankrupt. When government does it, it sends you the bill. And when government does it for 40 years, the bill comes in two ways: Higher taxes and inflation. Make no mistake about it. Inflation is a tax and not by accident. Lenin once said, "Through inflation government can quietly and unobservedly confiscate the prosperity of its citizens."

Speaking to the American Trucking Association Board of Directors, San Francisco, California, October 6, 1974

86

You know, some years ago there was an economist at Harvard, now deceased, Sumner Schlichter. And he said once that if a visitor from Mars came to earth, he would conclude that our tax policy had been created to make private enterprise unworkable.

Now some academicians have commented—well, they've referred to this as the *x* factor in human affairs, a confidence or a spirit that makes men and women dream and dare to greater risks. Well, for too long a time our tax structure has stifled that   factor and that spirit of confidence and daring in our economic doings here in our land.

Those who have the means to invest have sought tax shelters instead. And workers have been discharged from saving or even trying to increase their earnings by increasing their productivity. I think the people have told us they want to see America return to the can-do spirit that made this country an industrial and economic giant.

Remarks on the Program for Economic Recovery at a White House reception for Members of the House of Representatives, May 11, 1981

We always must ask: Is government working to liberate and empower the individual? Is it creating incentives for people to produce, save, invest, and profit from legitimate risks and honest toil? Is it encouraging all of us to reach for the stars? Or does it seek to compel, command, and coerce people into submission and dependence?

Ask these questions, because no matter where you look today, you will see that development depends on economic freedom.

Remarks at a luncheon of the World Affairs Council of Philadelphia, Pennsylvania, October 15, 1981

The main role of government is to provide a stable economic environment that allows each individual to reach his or her full potential. Individuals and businesses must be able to make long-run plans confident that the government will not change the rules halfway through the game. Government's drain on the economy, both through its resources that could be used more productively by the private sector and through taxes that destroy individual incentives, must be minimized. This Administration's long-term view of fiscal policy, which abandoned the outmoded emphasis on fine-tuning the economy, has set the basis for the record peacetime expansion we currently enjoy.

Letter to the Speaker of the House of Representatives and the President of the Senate Transmitting the Annual Economic Report of the President, January 10, 1989

We fear the government may be powerful enough to destroy families; we know that it is not powerful enough to replace them.

Speaking at the American Conservative Union Banquet, Washington D.C., February 6, 1977

We in government should learn to look at our country with the eyes of the entrepreneur, seeing possibilities where others see only problems.

Radio Address to the Nation on Economic Growth, January 26, 1985

Private business and industry is the most
over-regulated, over-taxed and, under-
appreciated part of America's society.

Address as Governor of California, 1974

" ... It is reported to us," the item said, "that the Lord's Prayer contains 57 words. Lincoln's Gettysburg Address has 266 words. The Ten Commandments are presented in just 297 words, and the Declaration of Independence has only 300 words." And then it goes on to say, " ... an Agriculture Department order setting the price of cabbage has 26,911 words."

Well, I thought you'd like to know we've had our researchers working around the clock to find that cabbage regulation. Possibly, the story is more folklore than fact. But whichever, I think it's one case where a bit of folklore can convey a lot of wisdom.

Remarks at the annual Washington Policy Meeting of the National Association of Manufacturers, March 18, 1982

There can be no prosperity or even freedom for our people if we ever abandon the competitive economic system that transformed this country into the strongest nation in the world.

Address as Governor of California, 1972

Enterprise zones offer a bold new means of invigorating economically crippled communities and improving the life of some of our most disadvantaged citizens. Rather than bureaucratic controls and regulations, a method that has failed, we seek to focus the vigor and innovation of the marketplace on these enclaves of despair. By reducing taxes, by eliminating unnecessary regulations while protecting the health, safety, and civil rights of our citizens, by improving local services, and by involving neighborhood organizations, we will begin to improve areas formerly written off as hopelessly depressed and provide jobs for those who need them the most ....

Clearly, decades of spending programs have done little more than subsidize the status quo and make wards of the government out of citizens who would rather have a job than a handout. It's time for us to find out if two of the most dynamic and constructive forces known to man—free enterprise and the profit motive—can be brought to play where government bureaucracy and social programs have failed.

Remarks on signing a Message to Congress transmitting Proposed Enterprise Zone Legislation, March 23, 1982

No country in history has ever long survived a tax burden that reached one third of its citizens' earnings. Indeed, the first signs of disintegration begin when the total tax burden hits 25 percent.

Address as Governor of California, 1973

He said there's a rising Tide of good Cheer and Joy in the land. We see new Zest in the economy every day. And all we need now is a bold Dash to Safeguard the gain we've made already. I said thanks and congratulated him on the Top Job that you're all doing in support of tax fairness.

Remarks to employees at the Ivorydale Soap manufacturing plant, St. Bernard, Ohio, October 3, 1985

My friends, some years ago, the federal government declared war on poverty and poverty won.

Address before a Joint Session of Congress on the State of the Union, January 25, 1988

89

There's a story about a fellow who was always asking Abraham Lincoln to give him a government job. And one day the news was that the Customs chief had died, and sure enough, this fellow shows up and asks President Lincoln if he could take that fellow's place. And Lincoln says, "It's fine with me if the undertaker doesn't mind."

Remarks to the employees of United States Precision Lens, Inc., Cincinnati, Ohio, August 8, 1988

If you take the various ways of helping people, the one with the least overhead is the private effort; next is the community or local effort, if [it] is a public effort, but the highest of all is the federal government.

In addition to that, trying to form rules and regulations that will fit all of the various problems around the country ignores the diversity of this land of ours.

Remarks at a breakfast meeting with representatives from the private sector engaged in volunteer work, September 21, 1981

Secretary [of Education] Bennett makes, I think, an interesting analogy. He says that if you serve a child a rotten hamburger in America, federal, state, and local agencies will investigate you, summon you, close you down, whatever. But if you provide a child with a rotten education, nothing happens, except that you're liable to be given more money to do it with. Well, we've discovered that money alone isn't the answer.

Remarks to the National Governors' Association, February 22, 1988

They have kind of a layaway plan for your lives which never changes. It's called, "Americans make, government takes."

Remarks at the National Conference of the National Federation of Independent Business, June 22, 1983

Do you remember back in the days when you thought that nothing could replace the dollar? Today it practically has!

Address as Governor of California, 1973

The United States is the world's oldest democratic government. And at my age, when I tell you something is the oldest in the world, you can take my word for it; I'm probably talking from personal experience.

Remarks and a Question and Answer Session with junior high school students, November 14, 1988

As Dave Stockman pointed out the other day, we're still subsidizing 95 million meals a day, providing $70 billion in health care to the elderly and poor, some 47 million people. Some 10 million or more are living in subsidized housing. And we're still providing scholarships for a million and a half students. Only here in this city of Oz would a budget this big and this generous be characterized as a miserly attack on the poor.

Remarks at the annual Conservative Political Action Conference Dinner, February 26, 1982

Heaven help us if government ever gets into the business of protecting us from ourselves.

Address to students as Governor of California, 1973

The finger-pointers and hand-wringers of today were the policy makers of yesterday, and they gave us economic stagflation and double-digit inflation. There was only one thing fair about their policies: They didn't discriminate; they made everyone miserable.

Remarks to the annual convention of the Concrete and Aggregates Industries Association, Chicago, Illinois, January 31, 1984

When government decides to solve something, we have learned to be wary. The cure may not always be worse than the disease, but it is usually bigger and it costs more.

Address as Governor of California, 1972

Excellence demands competition among students and among schools. And why not? We must always meet our obligation to those who fall behind without our assistance. But let's remember, without a race there can be no champion, no records broken, no excellence—in education or any other walk of life.

This freedom to choose what type of education is best for each child has contributed much to

America's reputation for excellence in education. Unfortunately, the high plane of literacy and the diversity of education we have achieved is threatened by policy makers who seem to prefer uniform mediocrity to the rich variety that has been our heritage.

Remarks to the National Catholic Education Association, Chicago, Illinois, April 15, 1982

If a bureaucrat had been writing the Ten Commandments, a simple rock slab would not have been near enough room.

Those simple rules would have read: "Thou Shalt Not, unless you feel strongly to the contrary, or for the following stated exceptions, see paragraphs 1-10 subsection #A."

Address as Governor of California, 1974

Now the question I ask about my welfare reform proposal is: Will it help people become self-sufficient and lead a full life, or will it keep them down in a state of dependency?

Radio Address to the Nation on Welfare Reform, August 1, 1987

In our nation today, government has grown too big, too complex, and possessed of what Cicero called the "arrogance of officialdom." Remote from the wishes of the people, it forgets that ours is a system of government by the consent of the governed—not the other way around.

Address as Governor of California, 1973

One of the things that is wrong with government is this idea that there is a certain group of people who will make a professional career out of government. That's fine but we also must always have an influx into government of people … citizens who say, "I owe the community something and therefore I will give one year, two years, three years, four or five years … a period out of my life to serve my community and bring to government the thinking of the man on the street, the people out here who sometimes say 'why is government doing this?' "

Address to students as Governor of California, 1973

93

94

The Great Society is great only in power, in size, and in cost. And so are the problems it set out to solve.

Speaking at the American Conservative Union Banquet, Washington D.C., February 6, 1977

Our New Beginning is a continuation of that beginning created two centuries ago when—for the first time in history—government, the people said, was not our master. It is our servant. Its only power: That which we the people allow it to have.

That system has never failed us, but for a time we failed the system. We asked things of government that government was not equipped to give. We yielded authority to the national government that properly belonged to the states or to local governments or to the people themselves. We allowed taxes and inflation to rob us of our earnings and savings and watched the great industrial machine that had made us the most productive people on earth slow down and the number of unemployed increase.

By 1980 we knew it was time to renew our faith, to strive with all our strength toward the ultimate in individual freedom, consistent with an orderly society.

We believed then and now: There are no limits to growth and human progress when men and women are free to follow their dreams. And we were right to believe that. Tax rates have been reduced, inflation cut dramatically, and more people are employed than ever before in our history.

Inaugural Address, January 21, 1985

I think the so-called conservative is today what was, in the classic sense, the liberal. The classical liberal, during the Revolutionary time, was a man who wanted less power for the king and more power for the people. He wanted people to have more say in the running of their lives and he wanted protection for the God-given rights of the people. He did not believe those rights were dispensations granted by the king to the people, he believed that he was born with them. Well, that today is the conservative.

Interview as Governor of California, 1973

I'm delighted to have this opportunity to be with you today. Actually, I was thinking on the way over that this is the second gathering of attorneys I've addressed in the last few months. When I spoke to the American Bar Association a short time ago, I said how disappointed I was that the White House counsel wouldn't let me accept the honorarium. I was really looking forward to the first time I ever talked to a group of lawyers and came home with the fee.

Remarks during a White House Briefing for United States Attorneys, October 21, 1985

95

Now, not everything we did can or should be measured in dollars and cents. "Justice is the end of government," wrote Alexis de Tocqueville.

Remarks to Administration officials on Domestic Policy, December 13, 1988

Government does not produce revenue. It consumes it.

Address as Governor of California, 1974

The challenge of statesmanship is to have the vision to dream of a better, safer world and the courage, persistence, and patience to turn that dream into reality.

Remarks to the United States Negotiating Team for the Nuclear and Space Arms Negotiations with the Soviet Union, March 8, 1985

THE CHALLENGE OF STATESMANSHIP

A leader, once convinced a particular course of action is the right one, must have the determination to stick with it and be undaunted when the going gets rough.

Address to Cambridge Union Society, Cambridge, England, December 5, 1990

When I took the oath of office, I pledged loyalty to only one special interest group: "We the people." Those people—neighbors and friends, shopkeepers and laborers, farmers and craftsmen—do not have infinite patience. As a matter of fact, some 80 years ago, Teddy Roosevelt wrote these instructive words in his first message to the Congress: "The American people are slow to wrath, but when their wrath is once kindled, it burns like a consuming flame." Well, perhaps that kind of wrath will be deserved if our answer to these serious problems is to repeat the mistakes of the past.

Address before a Joint Session of Congress on the Program for Economic Recovery, April 28, 1981

I told maybe some of you the other day in a talk that I know it's hard, it's hard when you're up to your armpits in alligators to remember you came here to drain the swamp.

Remarks at a White House reception for women appointees of the administration, February 10, 1982

America needs leaders, not labels.

Remarks at Herbert Hoover Library, West Branch, Iowa, August 8, 1992

They tell me I'm the most powerful man in the world. I don't believe that. Over there in that White House someplace there is a fellow that puts a piece of paper on my desk every day that tells me what I'm going to be doing every 15 minutes. He's the most powerful man in the world.

Referring to the Director of Presidential Scheduling, February 23, 1984

I understand that there are some 150 principals with us here today. I'm delighted you're here, but I have to confess to some mixed emotions. I remember on a number of occasions when I was sent to see the principal, and now the principals are coming to see me.

Remarks on presenting Awards for Excellence in Education, September 28, 1983

I've returned to the campus many times, always with great pleasure and warm nostalgia. Now, it just isn't true that I only came back this time to clean out my gym locker.

On one of those occasions, as you've been told, I addressed the graduating class here, " 'neath the elms," and was awarded an honorary degree. And at that time, I informed those assembled that while I was grateful for the honor, it added to a feeling of guilt I'd been nursing for 25 years, because I always figured the first degree they gave me was honorary.

… Oh, you'll have some regrets along with the happy memories. I let football and other extracurricular activities eat into my study time, with the result that my grade average was closer to the C level required for eligibility than it was closer to straight A's. And even now I wonder what I might have accomplished if I had studied harder.

Commencement Address, Eureka College, Eureka, Illinois, May 9, 1982

98

Wendell Phillips once said that "you can always get the truth from an American statesman after he has turned 70 or given up all hopes of the presidency."

Toast at the State Dinner for President Mohammed Hosni Mubarak of Egypt, January 28, 1988

Just for the record, I'm speaking in jest here. Of course, some of you think I've been doing that for eight years now.

Remarks at the Congressional Barbecue, September 15, 1988

So, it was our Republican Party that gave me a political home. When I signed up for duty, I didn't have to check my principles at the door. And I soon found out that the desire for victory did not overcome our devotion to ideals.

Remarks at the Republican National Convention in New Orleans, Louisiana, August 15, 1988

I remember a story back from my Jim Rhodes days, my governor days in California. I was on the way to the office one morning, had the car radio on. And there was a disc jockey on playing songs and so forth and suddenly, I heard him saying—now, we were having some problems at the time—I heard him saying something that endeared him to me. He said, "Every man should take unto himself a wife, because sooner or later, something is bound to happen that you can't blame on the governor."

Remarks to business leaders in Cincinnati, Ohio, October 3, 1985

99

Too often character assassination has replaced debate in principle here in Washington. Destroy someone's reputation, and you don't have to talk about what he stands for.

Remarks at the annual meeting of the National Alliance of Business, September 14, 1987

President Li comes from a nation whose people are known for their traditional respect for the elders. President Li, I can assure you I'm doing my best to reestablish that tradition in our own country.

Toast at the State Dinner for President Li Xiannian of China, July 23, 1985

Now, what about your generation? Well, we've only seen the beginning of what free and brave people can do. You've all heard, of course, and studied the Industrial Revolution. Well, today our nation is leading another revolution even more sweeping as it touches our lives. It's a revolution ranging from tiny microchips to voyages into the vast, dark reaches of space; from home computers that can put the great music and film and literature at a family's fingertips to new medical devices and methods of healing that

could add years to your lives and even enable the halt to walk and the blind to see.

Your generation stands on the verge of greater advances than humankind has ever known. I remember my disbelief when I was told one day of a communications satellite that could deliver the entire Encyclopedia Britannica in three seconds. But for you to take advantage of these staggering advances, and your children, too, we must forge an education system to meet the challenge of change. The Senator spoke eloquently about this. The sad fact is that system doesn't exactly exist today. Of course, there are many fine schools   this university is a notable example—and thousands of dedicated schoolteachers and administrators. But overall, lately, American schools have been failing to do the job they should.

Remarks at Convocation Ceremonies at the University of South Carolina, September 20, 1983

I've always wanted to be on a McLaughlin show. I was in the neighborhood and thought I'd just drop in. Let's cut the nonsense and get down to beltway business. Issue one: The McLaughlin Group, three

years running strong and getting stronger, seen in—well, you've just heard how many markets. And now we know that next year it's going to play the big towns. In just three short years, the McLaughlin Group has distinguished itself on three fronts. First, it became a stable—staple—that was a Freudian slip—in America's diet of political commentary. Its intellectual nutritional values fall somewhere between potato chips and Twinkies. Second, the McLaughlin Group also serves as the most tasteful programming alternative to professional wrestling live from Madison Square Garden. And third, it's also been an obedience school for White House staffers. Issue two, political potpourri: We're talking about the four horsemen of the political apocalypse and their now famous rotating chair. By the way, Pat Buchanan rotated all the way to a windowless office down the hall in the west wing just across from the broom closet.

Remarks at a reception for the McLaughlin Group, October 29, 1985

101

It's always wonderful to return to Eureka. People ask me if in looking back at my college years I can remember any inkling that I would someday run for President. Well, actually, the thought first struck me on graduation day when the president of the college handed me my diploma and asked, "Are you better off today than you were four years ago?"

Remarks at Eureka College, Eureka, Illinois, February 6, 1984

Q: Are you going to fire Don Regan?

A: [laughing] Are you talking about the Redskin football player?

Q: Not quite. I'm talking about *The Post* articles on the schism of your hierarchy.

A: If I fired anybody, it would be *The Post*.

Remarks and Question and Answer Session with reporters, September 9, 1985

On the return of the President to the Washington Hilton …

You know, I was speaking to that group last year. I've got to speak again.

Q: Do you have any fear and trepidation about going back?

A: No, but I'm wearing my oldest suit today.

Question and Answer Session with reporters on Domestic and Foreign Policy Issues, April 5, 1982

I can't help finding it hard to believe that this chapter in the American saga is about to end. Yes there are many things that I'll miss when I'm back at the ranch. The courtly courtesy of Sam Donaldson. The your-wish-is-our-command helpfulness of Congress. Yet as soon as I get home to California, I plan to lean back, kick up my feet, and take a long nap. Now, come to think of it, things won't be that different after all.

Remarks to Administration officials on Domestic Policy, December 13, 1988

Well, at this point in my career, I'm used to a certain amount of skepticism. Back in 1966, when somebody told my old boss, Jack Warner, that I was running for governor of California, he thought for a minute and said, "No, Jimmy Stewart for governor, Reagan for best friend."

Remarks at a White House briefing for state and local officials on the Economic Bill of Rights, July 22, 1987

Q: Mr. President, could you tell us when you will announce that you will seek or not seek the Presidency again?

A: At the last possible moment that I can announce a decision, and for a very obvious reason. Number one, if the answer is no, I'm a lame duck and can't get anything done. If the answer is yes, they'll charge that everything I'm doing is political— and I can't get anything done. So, I'm going to wait as long as I can.

Remarks and a Question and Answer Session with writers for hispanic, religious, and labor publications, September 14, 1983

You know, it wasn't so very long ago that all I had to do to start an unfriendly campus riot was show up. And now on campaign stop after campaign stop, in state after state, I've seen so many young Americans, like yourselves, coming out to say hello.

Remarks at a Republican Campaign Rally in Mount Clements, Michigan, November 5, 1988

As Henry VIII said to each of his six wives, "I won't keep you long."

Remarks and a Question and Answer Session with members of the American Business Conference, March 24, 1987

All I can tell you is I fought like a tiger against ever running for office. I thought that was for someone else, that I would do what I had done for other candidates, like my speeches for Barry Goldwater, that I would campaign for others. And when I was beset in 1965 by this group that insisted that I had to seek the governorship against the incumbent governor then because the party was divided and all, I fought like a tiger not to. And finally, I couldn't sleep nights, and Nancy and I said yes. But then, I have to tell you, we'd only been there a few months and one night we looked at each other, sitting in the living room in Sacramento, and said this makes everything else we've ever done look as dull as dishwater.

Interview with Hugh Sidey, Time Magazine, August 12, 1987

There are worse things to be called than a dreamer.

Address to Oxford Union Society, Oxford, England, December 4, 1992

103

We should be strong and courageous in our own embrace of democracy, as this is not the time to let our support for budding democracies wane. Which reminds me of a story I once heard:

A very wealthy man bought a huge ranch and he invited some of his closest associates to see it. After touring many acres of mountains and rivers and grasslands, he brought everybody back to the house for lunch. The house was spectacular and out back was the largest swimming pool you have ever seen. The strange thing was, however, that it was filled with alligators. The owner explained them by saying, "I value courage more than anything else. Courage is what made me a rich man. In fact, I think that courage is such a powerful virtue that if anybody is courageous enough to jump in that pool, swim through those alligators and make it to the other side, I'll give them anything they want, anything—my house, my land, my money. Of course everyone laughed at the absurd challenge and proceeded to follow the owner into the house for lunch. Suddenly they heard a splash. Turning around they saw this fellow swimming for his life across the pool, thrashing at the water, as the alligators swarmed after him. After several death-defying seconds, the man made it unharmed to the other side. The rich host was amazed, but stuck to his promise, saying, "You are indeed a man of courage and I will stick to my word. What do you want? You can have anything: My house, my land, my money. Just tell me what you want and it's yours." The swimmer, breathing heavily, looked up at his host and said, "I just want to know one thing—who the hell pushed me in that pool!?!"

Remarks at a reception honoring Chancellor and Mrs. Helmut Kohl of Germany at the home of Rupert and Anna Murdoch, Beverly Hills, California, September 15, 1991

Tip O'Neill once asked me how I keep myself looking so young for the cameras. I told him I have a good makeup team. It's the same people who've been repairing the Statue of Liberty.

Remarks at the annual White House News Photographers' Association Dinner, May 15, 1986

For you see, the character that takes command in moments of crucial choices has already been determined. It has been determined by a thousand other choices made earlier in seemingly unimportant moments. It has been determined by all the "little" choices of years past—by all those times when the voice of conscience was at war with the voice of temptation—whispering the lie that "it really doesn't matter." It has been determined by all the day-to-day decisions made when life seemed easy and crises seemed far away—the decision that, piece by piece, bit by bit, developed habits of discipline or of laziness; habits of self-sacrifice or of self-indulgence; habits of duty and honor and integrity—or dishonor and shame.

Remarks at Commencement Exercises, The Citadel, May 15, 1993

History's no easy subject. Even in my day it wasn't, and we had so much less of it to learn then.

Remarks to winners of the Bicentennial of the Constitution Essay Competition, September 10, 1987

104

I mean no irreverence when I mention that I once played a sheriff on TV who thought he could do the job without a gun. I was dead in the first 27 minutes of the show.

Remarks at the annual meeting of the International Association of Chiefs of Police, New Orleans, Louisiana, September 28, 1981

Once during the campaign some fellow said to me that he didn't think I was working very hard. He said, "You've got too good a tan." And I said, "Well, I've been doing a lot of outdoor rallies." And then he says, "Well, you talk too long then."

Remarks at a Republican Party Rally, Reno, Nevada, October 7, 1982

There are three stages of reaction to any new idea, as Arthur C. Clarke, a brilliant writer with a fine scientific mind, once noted. First, "It's crazy; don't waste my time." Second, "It's possible, but it's not worth doing." And finally, "I always said it was a good idea."

Remarks at a White House briefing for supporters of the Strategic Defense Initiative, August 6, 1986

I think I may have told some of you this before, but I've just come from Michigan, where I met with our friend from below the border, President Lopez Portillo, and it reminded me of this. I'm going to tell it again, just in case. And that was how I once addressed a very large, distinguished audience in Mexico City and sat down to rather scattered and unenthusiastic applause. And I was somewhat embarrassed, even more so when the next man who spoke, a representative of the Mexican government speaking in Spanish, which I don't understand, was being interrupted virtually every other line with the most enthusiastic kind of applause. To hide my embarrassment, I started clapping before anyone else and clapped longer than anyone else until our Ambassador leaned over and said to me, "I wouldn't do that if I were you; he's interpreting your speech."

Remarks at the Biennial Convention of the National Federation of Republican Women, Denver, Colorado, September 18, 1981

One thing our Founding Fathers could not foresee … they were farmers, professional men, businessmen giving of their time and effort to a dream and an idea that became a country … was a nation governed by professional politicians who had a vested interest in getting reelected. They probably envisioned a fellow serving a couple of hitches and then looking eagerly forward to getting back to the farm.

Interview as Governor of California, 1973

Last year, you all helped me begin celebrating the 31st anniversary of my 39th birthday. And I must say that all of those pile up, an increase of numbers, don't bother me at all, because I recall that Moses was 80 when God commissioned him for public service, and he lived to be 120. And Abraham was 100 and his wife, Sarah, 90 when they did something truly amazing—and he lived to be 175. Just imagine if he had put $2,000 a year into his IRA account.

Remarks at the annual National Prayer Breakfast, February 4, 1982

105

I'm sorry that some of the chairs on the left seem to be uncomfortable.

Address before the Assembly of the Republic of Portugal, as some of the Communist party assembly members walked out in protest of his address, May 9, 1985,

The crime problem has indeed become a matter of widespread concern, even among people of different philosophies. Today's hardliner on law and order is yesterday's liberal who was mugged last night.

Address as Governor of California, 1973

The reason there is a cynical lack of confidence in government is because too many politicans are elected to office but never try to carry out their campaign promises.

Address as Governor of California, 1974

Missed me!

Remarks at a Republican Party Rally, upon the inadvertent popping of a balloon, Omaha, Nebraska, October 21, 1982,

The members of Congress, I must say, were so friendly and warm last night that I almost said, "Why don't you pass everything now, and I'll sign it before I leave."

Remarks and a Question and Answer Session at a White House briefing for members of the Association of Independent Television Stations following the State of the Union Address, January 27, 1982

Now, there are some people who currently have plenty of time to run for office, but they don't seem to have any time for new ideas. Most of them are younger than I am. Everybody is. But I just have to call some of those young people I've been describing as the "old men of Washington," because their ideas are so old and threadbare.

Remarks at a ceremony marking the beginning of the Job Training Partnership Program, October 5, 1983

It's been the honor of my life to be your
President. So many of you have written the
past few weeks to say thanks, but I could
say as much for you. Nancy and I are grateful for the opportunity you gave us to serve.

Farewell Address to the Nation, January 11, 1989

And come January, when I saddle up and ride into the sunset it will be with the knowledge that we've done great things. We kept faith with a promise as old as this land we love and as big as the sky. A brilliant

WE KEPT FAITH

vision of America as a shining city on a hill. Thanks to all of you, and with God's help, America's greatest chapter is still to be written, for the best is yet to come.

Remarks at a dinner honoring Representative Jack F. Kemp of New York, December 1, 1988

I've always believed that we were, each of us, put here for a reason, that there is a plan, somehow a divine plan for all of us. I know now that whatever days are left to me belong to Him.

I also believe this blessed land was set apart in a very special way, a country created by men and women who came here not in the search of gold, but in search of God. They would be free people, living under the law with faith in their Maker and their future.

Remarks at the annual National Prayer Breakfast, February 4, 1982

110

We just celebrated the happiest and holiest holidays of the Christian faith, and we're in the sixth of the eight days of Passover, a reminder of our nation's Judeo-Christian tradition. Today, America's in the midst of a period of re-evaluation about the role of our fundamental institutions, what functions are within the proper sphere of government, which of those should be left at state and local levels, how much can government tax before it infringes on our citizens' freedom and damages the economy's ability to grow and prosper.

For some time now, I've been convinced that there is a great hunger on the part of our people for a spiritual revival in this land. There is a role for churches and temples … just as there has been throughout our history. They were once the center of community activity, the primary source of help for the less fortunate, with the churches that ran orphanages, homes for the elderly, other vital services. As late as 1935, at the depth of the Great Depression, a substantial portion of all charity was sponsored by religious institutions. And today, as we all know, the field seems to have been co-opted by government.

Remarks on Private Sector Initiatives at a White House luncheon for National Religious Leaders, April 13, 1982

We make a living by what we get, we make a life by what we give.

Remarks at Herbert Hoover Library, West Branch, Iowa, August 8, 1992

I've lived a long time, but I can't remember a time in my life when I didn't believe that prejudice and bigotry were the worst of sins. My mother was the kindest person I've ever known and truly believed that we are all brothers and sisters— children of God. My father was a rough, tough Irishman. He might not have expressed himself the way my mother did—but when that great motion picture classic "The Birth of a Nation" came to our small town, the two kids in town who didn't get to see it were me and my brother.

Remarks at a White House reception for the National Council of Negro Women, July 28, 1983

To our mothers, we owe our highest esteem, for it is from their gift of life that the flow of events begins that shapes our destiny. A mother's love, nurturing, and beliefs are among the strongest influences molding the development and character of our youngsters. As Henry Ward Beecher wrote, "What a mother sings to the cradle goes all the way down to the coffin."

Proclamation for Mother's Day, April 6, 1983

If America is to remain what God, in His wisdom, intended for it to be—a refuge, a safe haven for those seeking human rights—then we must once again extend the most basic human right to the most vulnerable members of the human family. We must commit ourselves to a future in which the right to life of every human being—no matter how weak, no matter how small, no matter how defenseless—is protected by our laws and public policy.

Proclamation for National Sanctity of Human Life Day, January 14, 1985

I know I've taken a long time here, but I know that this is a problem at your age: That you're thinking so hard, so many of you, what do I want to do? And don't let it bother you that you haven't made that decision yet. You'll change your mind many times before it comes— the right moment. But then when it comes, just knock on the door, whatever you've chosen to do, and ask until you find somebody that will let you in.

Remarks and Question and Answer Session with students at Suitland High School in Suitland, Maryland, January 20, 1988

When it comes to retirement, the criterion should be fitness for work, not year of birth. Our studies suggest that ending forced retirement based solely on age will have minimal consequences on the employment of other groups and will help to erase the unjust perception that persons over 70 are less productive than their fellow citizens. We know that many individuals have valuable contributions to make well beyond 70 years of age, and they should have the opportunity to do so if they desire.

Remarks on signing the Older Americans Month Proclamation, April 2, 1982

May each of you have the heart to conceive, the understanding to direct, and the hand to execute works that will leave the world a little better for your having been here.

Remarks at Herbert Hoover Library, West Branch, Iowa, August 8, 1992

Education is like a diamond with many facets: It includes the basic mastery of numbers and letters that give us access to the treasury of human knowledge, accumulated and refined through the ages; it includes technical and vocational training as well as instruction in science, higher mathematics, and humane letters. But no true education can leave out the moral and spiritual dimensions of human life and human striving. Only education that addresses this dimension can lead to that blend of compassion, humility, and understanding that is summed up in one word: Wisdom.

Proclamation for Education Day, USA, 1986, April 19, 1986

111

I know that some believe that voluntary prayer in schools should be restricted to a moment of silence. We already have the right to remain silent—we can take our Fifth Amendment.

Remarks to the annual convention of National Religious Broadcasters, January 30, 1984

Today our nation is at peace and is enjoying prosperity, but our need for prayer is even greater. We can give thanks to God for the ever-increasing abundance He has bestowed on us, and we can remember all those in our society who are in need of help, whether it be material assistance in the form of charity or simply a friendly word of encouragement. We are all God's handiwork, and it is appropriate for us as individuals and as a nation to call on Him in prayer.

National Day of Prayer Proclamation,
January 29, 1985

The date that you and we celebrate Christmas may be different. But the meaning and magnificence of what we celebrate—the divine birth of one man, hero, strong yet tender, Prince of Peace—is the same. This birth brought forth good tidings of great joy to all people. For unto us was born this day a Savior who is Christ the Lord.

Message on the Observance of Orthodox
Christmas, January 6, 1986

As I reflect on my life, I recall the fact that I am a simple man from modest beginnings. The Reagans of Illinois had little in material terms, that's for sure, but we were emotionally healthy beyond imagination. For we were Americans, young people in a young land with the best days ahead. We admired the pioneering spirit of this hopeful land where everyone has a chance to push out the boundaries of life. America has been very kind to me in my long and fulfilling life. What better time and place to thank this great country for its blessings on me than here today in "America's House."

Presidential Medal of Freedom Ceremony,
The White House, January 13, 1993

The bonding which takes place in college is unlike any other experience. My young friends, savor these moments. Keep the memories close to your heart. Cherish your family and your friends. As I learned years ago, we never really know what the future will bring.

Remarks at George Washington University,
March 28, 1991

I find my thoughts turning to my own mother, Nelle Reagan. She was a truly remarkable woman—ever so strong in her determination yet always tender, always giving of herself to others. She never found time in her life to complain; she was too busy living those values she sought to impart in my brother and myself. She was the greatest influence on my life, and as I think of her this weekend I remember the words of Lincoln, "All that I am, or hope to be, I owe to my mother."

Radio Address to the Nation on
Mother's Day, May 11, 1985

And I can't help but tell a little story I heard the other day about faith. A fellow fell off a cliff, and as he was falling grabbed a limb sticking out the side of the cliff and looked down 300 feet to the canyon floor below and then looked up and said, "Lord, if there's anyone up there, give me faith. Tell me what to do." And a voice from the heavens said, "If you have faith, let go." He looked down at the canyon floor and then took another look up and said, "Is there anyone else up there?"

Remarks on signing the Challenge Grant
Amendments, September 26, 1983

113

And I have to relate just a little personal experience here in closing. I remember one day I was sitting in the principal's office. I wasn't invited there for a social visit. And he said something that fortunately stuck in my mind, and I remembered. He said, "Reagan, I don't care what you think of me now. I'm only concerned with what you'll think of me 15 years from now." And I thank the Lord that I had the opportunity to tell him shortly before he died how I felt about him 15 years afterward, after that visit in his office. And he was a very great influence in my life.

Remarks on receiving the Department of Education Report on Improving Education, May 20, 1987

Talking to a church audience like this reminds me a little of a church in a little town in Illinois—Dixon, Illinois—that I used to attend as a boy. One sweltering Sunday morning in July, the minister told us he was going to preach the shortest sermon he had ever given. And then he said a single sentence: "If you think it's hot today, just wait."

Remarks at the annual convention of the National Association of Evangelicals, Columbus, Ohio, March 6, 1984

Each of us, each of you, is made in the most enduring, powerful image of Western civilization. We're made in the image of God, the image of God the Creator.

Remarks to citizens in Hambach, Federal Republic of Germany, May 6, 1985

Let us go forward with our conviction that education doesn't begin with Washington officials or state officials or local officials. It begins with the family, where it is the right and the responsibility of every parent. And that responsibility, I think, includes teaching children respect for skin color that is different from their own; religious beliefs that are different from their own. It includes conveying the message to the young as well as to the old that racial discrimination and religious bigotry have no place in a free society.

Remarks at the annual convention of National Religious Broadcasters, February 9, 1982

Prayer, of course, is deeply personal: The way in which it finds expression depends on our individual dispositions as well as on our religious convictions. Just as our religious institutions are guaranteed freedom in this land, so also do we cherish the diversity of our faiths and the freedom afforded to each of us to pray according to the promptings of our individual conscience.

Proclamation for National Day of Prayer, May 1, 1986

There must be higher yearning equal to or surpassing the higher learning. A university is a place where ancient tradition thrives alongside the most revolutionary of ideas. Perhaps as no other institution, a university is simultaneously committed to the day before yesterday and day after tomorrow.

Address to Oxford Union Society, Oxford, England, December 4, 1992

I never miss the chance to visit Philadelphia, America's historic treasure. For one thing, there aren't too many cities that have been around much longer than I have. You know, your own Ben Franklin once said, "Work as if you were to live a hundred years. Pray as if you were to die tomorrow." And ever since he told me that, I've been doing just fine.

Remarks at a fundraising luncheon for Governor Richard L. Thornburg, January 25, 1988

The First Continental Congress made its first act a prayer—the beginning of a great tradition. We have then, a lesson from the founders of our land, those giants of soul and intellect whose courageous pledge of life and fortune and sacred honor, and whose "firm reliance on the protection of Divine Providence," have ever guided and inspired Americans and all who would fan freedom's mighty flames and live in "freedom's holy light." That lesson is clear: That in the winning of freedom and in the living of life, the first step is prayer.

National Day of PrayerProclamation, February 3, 1988

Many of us have been taught to pray by people we love. In my case, it was my mother. I learned quite literally at her knee. My mother gave me a great deal, but nothing she gave me was more important than that special gift, the knowledge of the happiness and solace to be gained by talking to the Lord. The way we pray depends both on our religious convictions and our own individual dispositions, but the light of prayer has a common core. It is our hopes and our aspirations, our sorrows and fears, our deep remorse and renewed resolve, our thanks and joyful praise, and most especially our love, all turned toward a loving God.

Remarks on signing the 1987 National Day of Prayer Proclamation, December 22, 1986

The image of George Washington kneeling in prayer in the snow is one of the most famous in American history. He personified a people who knew it was not enough to depend on their own courage and goodness; they must also seek help from God, their Father and Preserver.

Christmas Radio Address to the Nation, December 24, 1983

Yours is a sacred mission. In the words of Henry Adams, "A teacher affects eternity." Each of you, as tiring and routine as your daily duties may sometimes seem, is a keeper of the American dream, the American future. By informing and exercising young minds, by transmitting learning and values, you are the vital link between all that is most precious in our national heritage and our children and grandchildren, who will some day take up the burdens of guiding the greatest, freest society on Earth.

Remarks at the annual convention of the American Federation of Teachers, Los Angeles, California, July 5, 1983

With freedom goes responsibility. Sir Winston Churchill once said you can have 10,000 regulations and still not have respect for the law. We might start with the Ten Commandments. If we lived by the Golden Rule, there would be no need for other laws.

Address as Governor of California, 1973

I have believed for a long time that we got off the track and our young people got off the track. And we saw a period in the generation gap where young people were discarding all the tried-and-true values upon which civilization has been based. And the only reason for discarding them was that they were old.

Remarks and a Question and Answer Session with women leaders of Christian religious organizations, October 13, 1983

118

Our forefathers drew on the wisdom and strength of God when they turned a vast wilderness into a blessed land of plenty called the United States of America. God has truly blessed this country, but we never should fall into the trap that would detract from the universality of God's gift. It is for all mankind. God's love is the hope and the light of the world.

Remarks at the Annual National Prayer Breakfast, February 4, 1988

The teaching of respect for the law cannot be left to education alone. It is a responsibility we all must assume, in our daily lives, in every school, in our churches, throughout our social structure.

Address as Governor of California, 1974

If Benjamin Franklin rose to invoke the Almighty as the Constitution itself was being drafted, if the Congress of the United States opens each day with prayer, then isn't it time we let God back into the classroom?

Remarks to the Student Congress on Evangelism, July 28, 1988

I grew up in a home where I was taught to believe in intercessory prayer. I know it's those prayers and millions like them that are building high and strong the cathedral of freedom that we call America, those prayers and millions like them that will always keep our country secure and make her a force for good in this too troubled world.

Remarks to the Student Congress on Evangelism, July 28, 1988

Here then is our formula for completing our crusade for freedom. Here is the strength of our civilization and our belief in the rights of humanity. Our faith is in a higher law. Yes, we believe in prayer and it's power. And like the Founding Fathers of both our lands, we hold that humanity was meant not to be dishonored by the all-powerful state, but to live in the image and likeness of Him who made us.

Remarks to members of the Royal Institute of International Affairs, London, England June 3, 1988

We pray for peace and for the devotion and strength of soul to build it and protect it always. We pray and we resolve to keep holy the memory of those who have died for our country and to make their cause inseparably our own. We pray and we promise, so that one day *Taps* will sound again for the young and the brave and the good.

Proclamation on Prayer for Peace, Memorial Day, May 21, 1987

The Constitution was never meant to prevent people from praying; its declared purpose was to protect their freedom to pray.

Radio Address to the Nation on Prayer, September 18, 1982

Here, too, one soon learns that so long as
books are kept open then minds can never
be closed.

Address to Oxford Union Society,
Oxford, England, December 4, 1992

Q: Well, I must say, twice you've been brushed by death since you've been in this office, and you seem unfazed. You keep going; you keep your hope up. What is it?

A: Well, I have a very real and deep faith. Probably, I'm indebted to my mother for that. And I figure that He will make a decision, and I can't doubt that whatever He decides will be the right decision.

Interview With Hugh Sidey, Time Magazine, *July 25, 1985*

We both deeply believed what it was we were espousing, but we were on opposite sides. And when we finished talking, as he rose he said, "I'm going out of here and do some praying." And I said, "Well, if you get a busy signal, it's me there ahead of you."

Remarks at the annual National Prayer Breakfast, February 4, 1982

And in closing, I'd like to say that many of my fellow hostages share with me the profound conviction that it was our Father, God, that brought us through this ordeal safely. And in the spirit of giving credit where credit is due, I just wonder if you'd join with me in a brief word of thanks to the Lord.

Our Father, we just gather before you in humble adoration and praise and thanks. For we know that it was your strong hands that held us safely through this ordeal, that gave us the courage and the strength to withstand the darkest times. And, so, Father, we just thank you for this, and we give you all the praise and the glory, through Jesus. Amen.

Remarks to the freed hostages from the Trans World Airlines hijacking incident, July 2, 1985

I think it'd be a tragedy for us to deny our children what the rest of us, in and out of government, find so valuable. If the President of the United States can pray with others in the Oval Office—and I have on a number of occasions—then let's make certain that our children have the same right as they go about preparing for their futures and for the future of this country.

Remarks at a candle-lighting ceremony for prayer in schools, September 25, 1982

Today, prayer is still a powerful force in America, and our faith in God is a mighty source of strength. Our Pledge of Allegiance states that we are "one nation under God," and our currency bears the motto, "In God We Trust."

The morality and values such faith implies are deeply embedded in our national character. Our country embraces those principles by design, and we abandon them at our peril. Yet in recent years, well-meaning Americans in the name of freedom have taken freedom away. For the sake of religious tolerance, they've forbidden religious practice in the classrooms. The law of this land has effectively removed prayer from our classrooms.

How can we hope to retain our freedom through the generations if we fail to teach our young that our liberty springs from an abiding faith in our Creator?

Remarks at a White House ceremony in observance of National Day of Prayer, May 6, 1982

The evidence of this is all around us. In the Declaration of Independence, alone, there are no fewer than four mentions of a Supreme Being. "In God We Trust" is engraved on our coinage. The Supreme Court opens its proceedings with a religious invocation. And the Congress opens each day with prayer from its chaplains. The schoolchildren of the United States are entitled to the same privileges as Supreme Court Justices and Congressmen. Join me in persuading the Congress to accede to the overwhelming desire of the American people for a constitutional amendment permitting prayer in our schools.

Remarks at the annual Conservative Political Action Conference Dinner, February 18, 1983

We Americans are blessed in so many ways. We're a nation under God, a living and loving God. But Thomas Jefferson warned us, "I tremble for my country when I reflect that God is just." We cannot expect Him to protect us in crisis if we turn away from Him in our everyday living. But you know, He

told us what to do in II Chronicles. Let us reach out to Him. He said, "If my people, which are called by my name, shall humble themselves and pray and seek my face and turn from their wicked ways, then will I hear from Heaven and will forgive their sin and will heal their land."

Remarks at a dinner honoring Senator Jesse Helms of North Carolina, June 16, 1983

The Founding Fathers believed that faith in God was the key to our being a good people and America's becoming a great nation. George Washington kissed the Bible at his inauguration. And to those who would have government separate from religion, he had these words: "Reason and experience both forbid us to expect that national morality can prevail in exclusion of religious principle." And Ben Franklin, at the time when they were struggling with what was to be the American Constitution, finally one day said to those who were working with him that, "Without God's help, we shall succeed in this political building no better than the builders of Babel."

Remarks and a Question and Answer Session with women leaders of Christian religious organizations, October 13, 1983

In this job of mine, you meet with so many people, deal with so many of the problems of man, you can't help being moved by the quiet, unknown heroism of all kinds of people—the Prime Minister of another country who makes the bravest of brave decisions that's right, but may not be too popular with his constituency; or the fellow from Indiana who writes to me about some problems he's been having and what he did to solve them.

You see the heroism and the goodness of man and know in a special way that we are all God's children. The clerk and the king and the communist were made in His image. We all have souls, and we all have the same problems. I'm convinced, more than ever, that man finds liberation only when he binds himself to God and commits himself to his fellow man.

Remarks at the annual National Prayer Breakfast, January 31, 1985

122

One hundred and fifty years ago, Alexis de Tocqueville found that all Americans believed that religious faith was indispensable to the maintenance of their republican institutions. Today, I join with the people of this Nation in acknowledging this basic truth, that our liberty springs from and depends upon an abiding faith in God.

Message to Congress transmitting the Proposed Constitutional Amendment on prayer in schools, March 8, 1983

During a trip to Ireland we visited Cashel Rock where St. Patrick is said to have raised the first cross. A young Irish guide was showing us through the ruins of an ancient cemetery. We came to a great tombstone and chiseled in the stone was an inscription. It read: "Remember me as you pass by, for as you are, so once was I. But as I am you, too, will be. So be content to follow me." That was too much for some Irishman who had scratched in the stone underneath, "To follow you I am content. I wish I knew which way you went."

Remarks at an Amoco Corporation Annual Conference, New Orleans, Louisiana, March 17, 1992

I have a very special old Bible. And alongside a verse in the Second Book of Chronicles there are some words, handwritten, very faded by now. And believe me, the person who wrote these words was an authority. Her name was Nelle Wilson Reagan. She was my mother. And she wrote about that verse, "A most wonderful verse for the healing of nations."

Now, the verse that she'd marked read: "If my people, which are called by my name, shall humble themselves, and pray, and seek my face, and turn from their wicked ways; then will I hear from heaven … and will heal their land."

I know at times all of us—I do—feel that perhaps in our prayers we ask for too much. And then there are other times when we feel that something isn't important enough to bother God with it. Maybe we should let Him decide those things.

Remarks at the annual National Prayer Breakfast, February 3, 1983

Through the storms of Revolution, Civil War, and the great World Wars, as well as during times of disillusionment and disarray, the nation has turned to God in prayer for deliverance. We thank Him for answering our call, for, surely, He has. As a nation, we have been richly blessed with His love and generosity.

National Day of Prayer Proclamation, February 12, 1982

In his remarks at Gettysburg, President Lincoln referred to ours as a "nation under God." We rejoice in the fact that, while we have maintained separate institutions of church and state over our 200 years of freedom, we have at the same time preserved reverence for spiritual beliefs. Although we are a pluralistic society, the giving of thanks can be a true bond of unity among our people. We can unite in gratitude for our individual freedoms and individual faiths. We can be united in gratitude for our nation's peace and prosperity when so many in this world have neither.

Proclamation on Thanksgiving Day, 1983

123

124

Whenever I consider the history of this nation, I'm struck by how deeply imbued with faith the American people were, even from the very first. Many of the first settlers came for the express purpose of worshipping in freedom. Historian Samuel Morrison wrote of one such group: "Doubting nothing and fearing no man, they undertook all to set all crooked ways straight and create a new Heaven and a new Earth. If they were not permitted to do that in England, they would find some other place to establish their city of God." Well, that place was this broad and open land we call America.

Remarks to the Student Congress on Evangelism, July 28, 1988

Our Nation's motto—"In God We Trust"—was not chosen lightly. It reflects a basic recognition that there is a divine authority in the universe to which this nation owes homage.

Throughout our history, Americans have put their faith in God, and no one can doubt that we have been blessed for it. The earliest settlers of this land came in search of religious freedom. Landing on a desolate shoreline, they established a spiritual foundation that has served us ever since.

It was the hard work of our people, the freedom they enjoyed and their faith in God that built this country and made it the envy of the world. In all of our great cities and towns evidence of the faith of our people is found: Houses of worship of every denomination are among the oldest structures.

While never willing to bow to a tyrant, our forefathers were always willing to get to their knees before God. When catastrophe threatened, they turned to God for deliverance. When the harvest was bountiful, the first thought was thanksgiving to God.

Prayer is today as powerful a force in our nation as it has ever been. We as a nation should never forget this source of strength. And while recognizing that the freedom to choose a Godly path is the essence of liberty, as a nation we cannot but hope that more of our citizens would, through prayer, come into a closer relationship with their Maker.

Proclamation on National Day of Prayer, March 19, 1981

I, too, have been described as an undying optimist, always seeing a glass half full when some see it as half empty. And, yes, it's true—I always see the sunny side of life. And that's not just because I've been blessed by achieving so many of my dreams. My optimism comes not just from my strong faith in God, but from my strong and enduring faith in man.

Remarks during the dedication of the Ronald Reagan Presidential Library, California, November 4, 1991

125

The war against drugs is a war of individual battles,
a crusade with many heroes, including America's
young people and also someone very special to me.
She has helped so many of our young people say no

NANCY ®

to drugs. Nancy, much credit belongs to you, and I
want to express to you your husband's pride and your
country's thanks. Surprised you, didn't I?

Address before a Joint Session of Congress on the State of the Union,
January 25, 1988

How do you explain it? We're happy. I don't know how to answer it. From a man's standpoint, I could say what I think Clark Gable once said to someone, "There's nothing more important than approaching your own doorstep and knowing that someone on the other side is listening for the sound of your footsteps."

I know that during the day, even before this job, whatever I was doing, something would happen in a day and the first thing that would go through my mind was picturing myself telling her about it when I got home.

We talk about everything. Sometimes, we disagree on someone or their particular qualifications or something, but never very seriously. It's good to talk about it and have other input. I feel better always knowing that we're in agreement.

Comments made during an interview with Chris Wallace for the book, First Lady

… **H**er very presence has captivated me for nearly forty-two years of marriage. Nancy Davis Reagan has led a remarkable life—as an adoring daughter, a loving mother, a devoted and sensitive partner, and a worthy ambassador for our country as First Lady. I have seen her cope bravely with life's most difficult challenges, exuding grace and dignity and strength. She served this country as First Lady with enormous conviction and dedicated herself to helping victims of poverty and drugs by giving hope to those who had none. I am so proud of this woman—proud of her many accomplishments; for making a difference in the lives of the afflicted around the world, for standing beside me through good times and challenging ones, and for being a role model for women everywhere. I can't imagine life without her.

Message to the Junior League of Los Angeles Tribute Dinner honoring Nancy Reagan, March, 1994

I've been thinking for several days about what exactly I wanted to say today and how to put Nancy's role in my life in perspective for you. But what do you say about someone who gives your life meaning? What do you say about someone who's always there with support and understanding, someone who makes sacrifices so that your life will be easier and more successful? Well, what you say is that you love that person and treasure her. I simply can't imagine the last eight years without her. The presidency wouldn't have been the joy it's been for me without her there beside me. And that second-floor living quarters in the White House would have seemed a big and lonely spot without her waiting for me every day at the end of the day. She once said that a President has all kinds of advisers and experts who look after his interests when it comes to foreign policy or the economy or whatever, but no one who looks after his needs as a human being. Well, Nancy has done that for me through recuperations and crises. Every President should be so lucky.

Remarks at the Republican National Convention Luncheon honoring Nancy Reagan, New Orleans, Louisiana, August 15, 1988

128

Sometimes, I think my life really began
when I met Nancy.

From An American Life *by Ronald Reagan*

132

Forty years ago I entered a world of happiness. Nancy moved into my heart filling an empty spot with her love. From the start, our marriage was like an adolescent's dream of what a marriage should be. And for forty years it has gotten more so with each passing day.

Coming home to her, (even in sunny California), is like coming out of the cold into a warm, firelit room. When we're at home I miss her if she even steps out of the room. For four decades we have been side by side, step by step, hand in hand.

When we visited the ruins of the Berlin Wall recently I thought with some satisfaction how our marriage had outlasted the Iron Curtain!

With Nancy, I soon realized, my life was complete. With her, nothing was impossible. I am always enchanted by the musical quality of her laughter. I frequently try some quip or silly remark just so I can hear that beautiful tune once again.

When I needed her most, she was with me. On a fateful day in March 1981, an assassin's bullet came within an inch of my heart. But perhaps it didn't come closer because Nancy was already there, in my heart, making it stronger. Her love washed away the pain. She rescued me, prodded me during the hard work of recovery, bringing me back to a normal and healthy life.

A close brush with death establishes a bond like no other. People may not realize it about someone in the shielded life of the White House, but Nancy felt deeply for the victims of poverty and drugs, a trait she inherited from her wonderful mother whom she worshiped and so did I . Nancy worked so hard on her "Just Say No" program and her Foster Grandparents program, traveling all over the country and the world, giving speeches and giving hope to those who had no hope. I will never forget the pride I felt seeing Nancy meeting with world leaders and the Pope to discuss the international drug problem.

I always try to be there for the woman who has given so much to me. She lost both her parents when she was First Lady. I was very fond of them, and quite grateful they produced such a wonderful daughter. In fact, whenever Nancy's birthday came, I sent my mother-in-law flowers. I also removed the mother-in-law jokes from my speeches!

I remember holding Nancy's hand as we whispered prayers when she battled cancer. From the mail we got, we could see her courage inspired many other Americans who fought the dreaded disease. In turn, their outpouring of affection helped Nancy with her own struggle.

Recently, our pride and joy has been building the Ronald Reagan Presidential Library near Los Angeles. Five U.S. Presidents, past and present, attended the dedication ceremony on a beautiful sunny day last November. The American public can visit the library with its wealth of historic documents, its extensive exhibits, plus a huge chunk of the Berlin Wall. The library is special to me as a reminder of the many things Nancy and I have done together over the last forty years. The library is not only a fine record of the past, but a permanent monument to our everlasting love. I'll always be grateful that Nancy was at my side along my chosen trails.

Tribute to Nancy Reagan on their 40th Wedding Anniversary, March 6, 1992

Some may try and tell us that this is the end of an era. But what they overlook is that in America, every day is a new beginning, and every sunset is merely the latest milestone on a voyage that never ends. For

M ILESTONES

this is the land that has never become, but is always in the act of becoming. Emerson was right: America is the Land of Tomorrow.

Presidential Medal of Freedom Ceremony, The White House, January 13, 1993

Televised Nationwide Address on behalf of Senator Barry Goldwater, October 27, 1964

Announcer: The following prerecorded political program is sponsored for TV by Goldwater-Miller on behalf of Barry Goldwater, Republican candidate for President of the United States. Ladies and gentlemen, we take pride in presenting a thoughtful address by Ronald Reagan. Mr. Reagan …

Thank you very much. Thank you and good evening. The sponsor has been identified, but unlike most

television programs, the performer hasn't been provided with a script. As a matter of fact, I have been permitted to choose my own words and discuss my own ideas regarding the choice that we face in the next few weeks.

I have spent most of my life as a Democrat. I recently have seen fit to follow another course. I believe that the issues confronting us cross party lines. Now, one side in this campaign has been telling us that the issues of this election are the maintenance of peace and prosperity. The line has been used "We've never had it so good."

But I have an uncomfortable feeling that this prosperity isn't

WHERE IT ALL BEGAN

something upon which we can base our hopes for the future. No nation in history has ever survived a tax burden that reached a third of its national income. Today, 37 cents out of every dollar earned in this country is the tax collector's share, and yet our government continues to spend 17 million dollars a day more than the government takes in. We haven't balanced our budget 28 out of the last 34 years. We have raised our debt limit three times in the last twelve months, and now our national debt is one and a half times bigger than all the combined debts of all the nations of the world. We have 15 billion dollars in gold in our treasury—we don't own an ounce. Foreign dollar claims are 27.3 billion dollars, and we have just had announced that the dollar of 1939 will now purchase 45 cents in its total value.

As for the peace that we would preserve, I wonder who among us would like to approach the wife or mother whose husband or son has died in Vietnam and ask them if they think this is a peace that should be maintained indefinitely. Do they mean peace, or do they mean we just want to be left in peace? There can be no real peace while one American is dying some place in the world for the rest of us. We are at war with the most

dangerous enemy that has ever faced mankind in his long climb from the swamp to the stars, and it has been said if we lose that war, and in doing so lose this way of freedom of ours, history will record with the greatest astonishment that those who had the most to lose did the least to prevent its happening. Well, I think it's time we ask ourselves if we still know the freedoms that were intended for us by the Founding Fathers.

Not too long ago two friends of mine were talking to a Cuban refugee, a businessman who had escaped from Castro, and in the midst of his story one of my friends turned to the other and said, "We don't know how lucky we are." And the Cuban stopped and said, "How lucky you are! I had someplace to escape to." In that sentence he told us the entire story. If we lose freedom here, there is no place to escape to.

This is the last stand on earth.

And this idea that government is beholden to the people, that it has no other source of power except the sovereign people, is still the newest and most unique idea in all the long history of man's relation to man. This is the issue of this election. Whether we believe in our capacity for self-government or whether we abandon the American revolution and confess that a little intellectual elite in a far-distant capital can plan our lives for us better than we can plan them ourselves.

You and I are told increasingly that we have to choose between a left or right, but I would like to suggest that there is no such thing as a left or right. There is only an up or down—up to man's age-old dream, the ultimate in individual freedom consistent with law and order—or down to the ant heap of totalitarianism, and regardless of their sincerity, their humanitarian motives, those who would trade our freedom for security have embarked on this downward course.

In this vote-harvesting time, they use terms like the "Great Society," or as we were told a few days ago by the President, we must accept a "greater government activity in the affairs of the people." But they have been a little more explicit in the past and among themselves—and all of the things that I now will quote have appeared in print. These are not Republican accusations. For example, they have voices that say "the cold war will end through acceptance of a not undemocratic socialism." Another voice says that the profit motive has become outmoded, it must be replaced by the incentives of the welfare state; or our traditional system of individual freedom is incapable of solving the complex problems of the twentieth century.

Senator Fulbright has said at Stanford University that the Constitution is outmoded. He referred to the president as our moral teacher and our leader, and he said he is hobbled in his task by the restrictions in power imposed on him by this antiquated document. He must be freed so that he can do for us what he knows is best.

And Senator Clark of Pennsylvania, another articulate spokesman, defines liberalism as "meeting the material needs of the masses through the full power of centralized government." Well, I for one resent it when a representative of the people refers to you and me—the free men and women of this country—as "the masses." This is a term we haven't applied to ourselves in America. But beyond that, "the full power of centralized government"—this was the very thing the Founding Fathers sought to minimize. They knew that governments don't control things. A government can't control the economy without controlling people. And they know when a government sets out to do that, it must use force and coercion to achieve its purpose. They also knew, those Founding Fathers, that outside of its legitimate functions, government does nothing as well or as economically as the private sector of the economy.

139

Now, we have no better example of this than the government's involvement in the farm economy over the last thirty years. Since 1955, the cost of this program has nearly doubled. One-fourth of farming in America is responsible for 85 percent of the farm surplus. Three-fourths of farming is out on the free market and has known a 21 percent increase in the per capita consumption of all its produce. You see, that's one-fourth of farming that's regulated and controlled by the federal government. In the last three years we have spent $43 in the feed grain program for every dollar bushel of corn we don't grow.

Senator Humphrey last week charged that Barry Goldwater as President would seek to eliminate farmers. He should do his homework a little better, because he will find out that we have had a decline of five million in the farm population under these government programs. He will also find that the Democratic administration has sought to get from Congress an extension of the farm program to include that three-fourths that is now free. He will find that they have also asked for the right to imprison farmers who wouldn't keep books as prescribed by the federal government. The secretary of agriculture asked for the right to seize farms through condemnation and resell them to other individuals. And contained in that same program was a provision that would have allowed the federal government to remove two million farmers from the soil.

At the same time, there has been an increase in the Department of Agriculture employees. There is now one for every thirty farms in the United States, and still they can't tell us how 66 shiploads of grain headed for Austria disap-peared without a trace, and Billie Sol Estes never left shore.

Every responsible farmer and farm organization has repeatedly asked the government to free the farm economy, but who are farmers to know what is best for them? The wheat farmers voted against a wheat program. The government passed it anyway. Now the price of bread goes up; the price of wheat to the farmers goes down.

* * *

Meanwhile, back in the city, under urban renewal the assault on freedom carries on. Private property rights are so diluted that public interest is almost anything that a few government planners decide it should be. In a program that takes for the needy and gives to the greedy, we see such spectacles as in Cleveland, Ohio, a million-and-a-half-dollar building completed only three years ago must be destroyed to

140

make way for what government officials call a "more compatible use of the land." The President tells us he is now going to start building public housing units in the thousands where heretofore we have only built them in the hundreds. But FHA and the Veterans Administration tell us that they have 120,000 housing units they've taken back through mortgage foreclosures.

For three decades, we have sought to solve the problems of unemployment through government planning, and the more the plans fail, the more the planners plan. The latest is the Area Redevelopment Agency. They have just declared Rice County, Kansas, a depressed area. Rice County, Kansas, has two hundred oil wells, and the 14,000 people there have over thirty million dollars on deposit in personal savings in their banks. When the government tells you you are depressed, lie down and be depressed!

We have so many people who can't see a fat man standing beside a thin one without coming to the conclusion that the fat man got that way by taking advantage of the thin one. So they are going to solve all the problems of human misery through government and government planning. Well, now, if government planning and welfare had the answer and they've had almost thirty years of it, shouldn't we expect government to almost read the score to us once in a while? Shouldn't they be telling us about the decline each year in the number of people needing help? The reduction in the need for public housing?

But the reverse is true. Each year the need grows greater, the program grows greater. We were told four years ago that 17 million people went to bed hungry each night. Well, that was probably true. They

were all on a diet. But now we are told that 9.3 million families in this country are poverty-stricken on the basis of earning less than $3,000 a year. Welfare spending is ten times greater than in the dark depths of the Depression. We are spending 45 billion dollars on welfare. Now do a little arithmetic, and you will find that if we divided the 45 billion dollars up equally among those 9 million poor families, we would be able to give each family $4,600 a year, and this added to their present income should eliminate poverty! Direct aid to the poor, however, is running only about $600 per family. It seems that someplace there must be some overhead.

So now we declare "war on poverty," or "you, too, can be a Bobby Baker!" How do they honestly expect us to believe that if we add one billion dollars to the 45 billion we are spending … one more

141

program to the 30-odd we have—and remember, this new program doesn't replace any, it just duplicates existing programs … do they believe that poverty is suddenly going to disappear by magic? Well, in all fairness I should explain that there is one part of the new program that isn't duplicated. This is the youth feature. We are now going to solve the dropout problem, juvenile delinquency, by reinstituting something like the old CCC camps, and we are going to put our young people in camps, but again we do some arithmetic, and we find that we are going to spend each year just on room and board for each young person that we help $4,700 a year! We can send them to Harvard for $2,700! Don't get me wrong. I'm not suggesting that Harvard is the answer to juvenile delinquency.

But seriously, what are we doing to those we seek to help? Not too

long ago, a judge called me here in Los Angeles. He told me of a young woman who had come before him for a divorce. She had six children, was pregnant with her seventh. Under his questioning, she revealed her husband was a laborer earning $250 a month. She wanted a divorce so that she could get an $80 raise. She is eligible for $330 a month in the Aid to Dependent Children Program. She got the idea from two women in her neighborhood who had already done that very thing.

Yet anytime you and I question the schemes of the do-gooders, we are denounced as being against their humanitarian goals. They say we are always "against" things, never "for" anything. Well, the trouble with our liberal friends is not that they are ignorant, but that they know so much that isn't so. We are for a provision that destitution should not follow unemployment by reason of

old age, and to that end we have accepted social security as a step toward meeting the problem.

But we are against those entrusted with this program when they practice deception regarding its fiscal shortcomings, when they charge that any criticism of the program means that we want to end payments to those people who depend on them for livelihood. They have called it insurance to us in a hundred million pieces of literature. But then they appeared before the Supreme Court and they testified that it was a welfare program. They only use the term "insurance" to sell it to the people. And they said Social Security dues are a tax for the general use of the government, and the government has used that tax. There is no fund, because Robert Byers, the actuarial head, appeared before a congressional committee and admitted that Social Security as

143

of this moment is $298 billion in the hole. But he said there should be no cause for worry because as long as they have the power to tax, they could always take away from the people whatever they needed to bail them out of trouble! And they are doing just that.

A young man, 21 years of age, working at an average salary ... his social security contribution would, in the open market, buy him an insurance policy that would guarantee $220 a month at age 65. The government promises 127. He could live it up until he is 31 and then take out a policy that would pay more than Social Security. Now, are we so lacking in business sense that we can't put this program on a sound basis so that people who do require those payments will find that they can get them when they are due ... that the cupboard isn't bare? Barry Goldwater thinks we can.

At the same time, can't we introduce voluntary features that would permit a citizen to do better on his own, to be excused upon presentation of evidence that he had made provisions for the non-earning years? Should we not allow a widow with children to work, and not lose the benefits supposedly paid for by her deceased husband? Shouldn't you and I be allowed to declare who our beneficiaries will be under these programs, which we cannot do? I think we are for telling our senior citizens that no one in this country should be denied medical care because of a lack of funds. But I think we are against forcing all citizens, regardless of need, into a compulsory government program, especially when we have such examples, as announced last week, when France admitted that their medicare program was now bankrupt. They've come to the end of the road.

In addition, was Barry Goldwater so irresponsible when he suggested that our government give up its program of deliberate planned inflation so that when you do get your social security pension, a dollar will buy a dollar's worth, and not 45 cents' worth?

I think we are for the international organization, where the nations of the world can seek peace. But I think we are against subordinating American interests to an organization that has become so structurally unsound that today you can muster a two-thirds vote on the floor of the General Assembly among the nations that represent less than 10 percent of the world's population. I think we are against the hypocrisy of assailing our allies because here and there they cling to a colony, while we engage in a conspiracy of silence and never open our mouths about the millions of

144

people enslaved in Soviet colonies in the satellite nations.

I think we are for aiding our allies by sharing of our material blessings with those nations which share in our fundamental beliefs, but we are against doling out money government to government, creating bureaucracy, if not socialism, all over the world. We set out to help 19 countries. We are helping 107. We spent $146 billion. With that money, we bought a $2 million dollar yacht for Haile Selassie. We bought dress suits for Greek undertakers, extra wives for Kenyan government officials. We bought a thousand TV sets for a place where they have no electricity. In the last six years, 52 nations have bought $7 billion of our gold, and all 52 are receiving foreign aid from us.

* * *

No government ever voluntarily reduces itself in size. Government programs, once launched, never disappear. Actually, a government bureau is the nearest thing to eternal life we'll ever see on this earth. Federal employees number 2.5 million, and federal, state, and local, one out of six of the nation's work force is employed by the government. These proliferating bureaus with their thousands of regulations have cost us many of our constitutional safeguards. How many of us realize that today federal agents can invade a man's property without

145

a warrant? They can impose a fine without a formal hearing, let alone a trial by jury, and they can seize and sell his property in auction to enforce the payment of that fine. In Chicot County, Arkansas, James Wier overplanted his rice allotment. The government obtained a $17,000 judgment, and a U.S. marshal sold his 950-acre farm at auction. The government said it was necessary as a warning to others to make the system work. Last February 19, at the University of Minnesota, Norman Thomas, six-time candidate for President on the Socialist Party ticket, said, "If Barry Goldwater became President, he would stop the advance of socialism in the United States." I think that's exactly what he will do.

As a former Democrat, I can tell you Norman Thomas isn't the only man who has drawn this parallel to socialism with the present adminis-

tration. Back in 1936, Mr. Democrat himself, Al Smith, the great American, came before the American people and charged that the leadership of his party was taking the part of Jefferson, Jackson, and Cleveland down the road under

the banners of Marx, Lenin, and Stalin. And he walked away from his party, and he never returned to the day he died, because to this day, the leadership of that party has been taking that party, that honorable party, down the road in the image of

the labor socialist party of England. Now it doesn't require expropriation or confiscation of private property or business to impose socialism upon a people. What does it mean whether you hold the deed or the title to your business or property if the government holds the power of life and death over that business or property? Such machinery already exists. The government can find some charge to bring against any concern it chooses to prosecute. Every businessman has his own tale of harassment. Somewhere a perversion has taken place. Our natural, inalienable rights are now considered to be a dispensation from government, and freedom has never been so fragile, so close to slipping from our grasp as it is at this moment. Our Democratic opponents seem unwilling to debate these issues. They want to make you and I think that this is a contest between two men … that we are to choose

just between two personalities.

Well, what of this man they would destroy? And in destroying, they would destroy that which he represents, the ideas that you and I hold dear. Is he the brash and shallow and trigger-happy man they say he is? Well, I have been privileged to know him "when." I knew him long before he ever dreamed of trying for high office, and I can tell you personally I have never known a man in my life I believe so incapable of doing a dishonest or dishonorable thing.

This is a man who in his own business, before he entered politics, instituted a profit-sharing plan, before unions had ever thought of it. He put in health and medical insurance for all his employees. He took 50 percent of the profits before taxes and set up a retirement plan, and a pension plan for all his employees. He sent checks for life to an employee who was ill and couldn't

work. He provided nursing care for the children of mothers who work in the stores. When Mexico was ravaged by the floods from the Rio Grande, he climbed in his airplane and flew medicine and supplies down there.

An ex-GI told me how he met him. It was the week before Christmas during the Korean War, and he was at the Los Angeles airport trying to get a ride home to Arizona, and he said that there were a lot of servicemen there and no seats available on the planes. Then a voice came over the loudspeaker and said, "Any men in uniform wanting a ride to Arizona, go to runway such-and-such," and they went down there, and there was this fellow named Barry Goldwater sitting in his plane. Every day in the weeks before Christmas, all day long, he would load up the plane, fly to Arizona, fly them to their

147

homes, then fly back over to get another load.

During the hectic split-second timing of a campaign, this is a man who took time out to sit beside an old friend who was dying of cancer. His campaign managers were understandably impatient, but he said, "There aren't many left who care what happens to her. I'd like her to know that I care." This is a man who said to his 19-year-old son, "There is no foundation like the rock of honesty and fairness, and when you begin to build your life upon that rock, with the cement of the faith in God that you have, then you have a real start." This is not a man who could carelessly send other people's sons to war. And that is the issue of this campaign that makes all of the other problems I have discussed academic, unless we realize that we are in a war that must be won.

Those who would trade our freedom for the soup kitchen of the welfare state have told us that they have a utopian solution of peace without victory. They call their policy "accommodation." And they say if we only avoid any direct confrontation with the enemy, he will forget his evil ways and learn to love us. All who oppose them are indicted as warmongers. They say we offer simple answers to complex problems. Well, perhaps there is a simple answer … not an easy one … but a simple one.

If you and I have the courage to tell our elected officials that we want our national policy based upon what we know in our hearts is morally right. We cannot buy our security, our freedom from the threat of the bomb by committing an immorality so great as saying to a billion now in slavery behind the Iron Curtain, "Give up your dreams

of freedom because to save our own skin, we are willing to make a deal with your slave masters." Alexander Hamilton said, "A nation which can prefer disgrace to danger is prepared for a master, and deserves one." Let's set the record straight. There is no argument over the choice between peace and war, but there is only one guaranteed way you can have peace … and you can have it in the next second … surrender.

Admittedly there is a risk in any course we follow other than this, but every lesson in history tells us that the greater risk lies in appeasement, and this is the specter our well-meaning liberal friends refuse to face … that their policy of accommodation is appeasement, and it gives no choice between peace and war, only between fight or surrender. If we continue to accommodate, continue to back and retreat, eventually we have to face the final demand—the ultimatum. And what then? When Nikita Khrushchev has told his people he knows what our answer will be? He has told them that we are retreating under the pressure of the Cold War, and someday when the time comes to deliver the ultimatum, our surrender will be voluntary because by that time we will have been weakened from within spiritually, morally, and economically. He believes this because from our side he has heard voices pleading for "peace at any price" or "better Red than dead," or as one commentator put it, he would rather "live on his knees than die on his feet." And therein lies the road to war, because those voices don't speak for the rest of us. You and I know and do not believe that life is so dear and peace so sweet as to be purchased at the price of chains and slavery. If nothing in life is worth dying for, when did this

begin—just in the face of this enemy? Or should Moses have told the children of Israel to live in slavery under the pharaohs? Should Christ have refused the cross? Should the patriots at Concord Bridge have thrown down their guns and refused to fire the shot heard 'round the world? The martyrs of history were not fools, and our honored dead who gave their lives to stop the advance of the Nazis didn't die in vain. Where, then, is the road to peace? Well, it's a simple answer after all.

You and I have the courage to say to our enemies, "There is a price we will not pay." There is a point beyond which they must not advance. This is the meaning in the phrase of Barry Goldwater's "peace through strength." Winston Churchill said that "the destiny of man is not measured by material computation. When great forces are

on the move in the world, we learn we are spirits—not animals." And he said, "There is something going on in time and space, and beyond time and space, which, whether we like it or not, spells duty."

You and I have a rendezvous with destiny. We will preserve for our children this, the last best hope of man on earth, or we will sentence them to take the last step into a thousand years of darkness.

We will keep in mind and remember that Barry Goldwater has faith in us. He has faith that you and I have the ability and the dignity and the right to make our own decisions and determine our own destiny.

Thank you.

149

Inaugural Address
January 20, 1981

Senator Hatfield, Mr. Chief Justice, Mr. President, Vice President Bush, Vice President Mondale, Senator Baker, Speaker O'Neill, Reverend Moomaw, and my fellow citizens:

To a few of us here today this is a solemn and most momentous occasion, and yet in the history of our nation it is a commonplace occurrence. The orderly transfer of authority as called for in the Constitution routinely takes place, as it has for almost two centuries, and few of us stop to think how unique we really are. In the eyes of many in the world, this every-four-year ceremony we accept as normal is nothing less than a miracle.

Mr. President, I want our fellow citizens to know how much you did to carry on this tradition. By your gracious cooperation in the transition process, you have shown a watching world that we are a united people pledged to maintaining a political system which guarantees individual liberty to a greater degree than any other, and I thank you and your people for all your help in maintaining the continuity which is the bulwark of our Republic.

The business of our nation goes forward. These United States are confronted with an economic affliction of great proportions. We suffer from the longest and one of the worst sustained inflations in our national history. It distorts our economic decisions, penalizes thrift, and crushes the struggling young and the fixed-income elderly alike. It threatens to shatter the lives of millions of our people.

Idle industries have cast workers into unemployment, human misery, and personal indignity. Those who do work are denied a fair return for their labor by a tax system which penalizes successful achievement and keeps us from maintaining full productivity.

But great as our tax burden is, it has not kept pace with public spending. For decades we have piled deficit upon deficit, mortgaging our future and our children's future for the temporary convenience of the present. To continue this long trend is to guarantee tremendous social, cultural, political, and economic upheavals.

You and I, as individuals, can, by borrowing, live beyond our means, but for only a limited period of time. Why, then, should we think that collectively, as a nation, we're not bound by that same limitation? We must act today in order to preserve tomorrow. And let there be no misunderstanding: We are going to begin to act, beginning today.

ENTERING THE WHITE HOUSE

151

The economic ills we suffer have come upon us over several decades. They will not go away in days, weeks, or months, but they will go away. They will go away because we as Americans have the capacity now, as we've had in the past, to do whatever needs to be done to preserve this last and greatest bastion of freedom.

In this present crisis, government is not the solution to our problem; government is the problem. From time to time we've been tempted to believe that society has become too complex to be managed by self-rule, that government by an elite group is superior to government for, by, and of the people. Well, if no one among us is capable of governing himself, then who among us has the capacity to govern someone else? All of us together, in and out of government, must bear the burden. The solutions we seek must be equitable, with no one group singled out to pay a higher price.

We hear much of special interest groups. Well, our concern must be for a special interest group that has been too long neglected. It knows no sectional boundaries or ethnic and racial divisions, and it crosses political party lines. It is made up of men and women who raise our food, patrol our streets, man our mines and factories, teach our children, keep our homes, and heal us when we're sick—professionals, industrialists, shopkeepers, clerks, cabbies, and truck drivers. They are, in short, "We the people," this breed called Americans.

Well, this administration's objective will be a healthy, vigorous, growing economy that provides equal opportunities for all Americans, with no barriers born of bigotry or discrimination. Putting America back to work means putting all Americans back to work. Ending inflation means freeing all Americans from the terror of runaway living costs. All must share in the productive work of this "new beginning," and all must share in the bounty of a revived economy. With the idealism and fair play which are the core of our system and our strength, we can have a strong and prosperous America, at peace with itself and the world.

So, as we begin, let us take inventory. We are a nation that has a government—not the other way around. And this makes us special among the nations of the Earth. Our government has no power except that granted it by the people. It is time to check and reverse the growth of government, which shows signs of having grown beyond the consent of the governed.

It is my intention to curb the

size and influence of the Federal establishment and to demand recognition of the distinction between the powers granted to the Federal government and those reserved to the States or to the people. All of us need to be reminded that the Federal government did not create the States; the States created the Federal government.

Now, so there will be no misunderstanding, it's not my intention to do away with government. It is rather to make it work—work with us, not over us; to stand by our side, not ride on our back. Government

can and must provide opportunity, not smother it; foster productivity, not stifle it.

If we look to the answer as to why for so many years we achieved so much, prospered as no other people on Earth, it was because here in this land we unleashed the energy and individual genius of man to a greater extent than has ever been done before. Freedom and the dignity of the individual have been more available and assured here than in any other place on Earth. The price for this freedom at times has been high, but we have

never been unwilling to pay that price.

It is no coincidence that our present troubles parallel and are proportionate to the intervention and intrusion in our lives that result from unnecessary and excessive growth of government. It is time for us to realize that we're too great a nation to limit ourselves to small dreams. We're not, as some would have us believe, doomed to an inevitable decline. I do not believe in a fate that will fall on us no matter what we do. I do believe in a fate that will fall on us if we do

153

nothing. So, with all the creative energy at our command, let us begin an era of national renewal. Let us renew our determination, our courage, and our strength. And let us renew our faith and our hope.

We have every right to dream heroic dreams. Those who say that we're in a time when there are no heroes, they just don't know where to look. You can see heroes every day going in and out of factory gates. Others, a handful in number, produce enough food to feed all of us and then the world beyond. You meet heroes across a counter, and they're on both sides of that counter. There are entrepreneurs with faith in themselves and faith in an idea who create new jobs, new wealth and opportunity. They're individuals and families whose taxes support the government and whose voluntary gifts support church, charity, culture, art, and education. Their patriotism is quiet, but deep. Their values sustain our national life.

Now, I have used the words "they" and "their" in speaking of these heroes. I could say "you" and "your," because I'm addressing the heroes of whom I speak—you, the citizens of this blessed land. Your dreams, your hopes, your goals are going to be the dreams, the hopes, and the goals of this administration, so help me God.

We shall reflect the compassion that is so much a part of your makeup. How can we love our country and not love our countrymen; and loving them, reach out a hand when they fall, heal them when they're sick, and provide opportunity to make them self-sufficient so they will be equal in fact and not just in theory?

Can we solve the problems confronting us? Well, the answer is an unequivocal and emphatic "yes." To paraphrase Winston Churchill, I did not take the oath I've just taken with the intention of presiding over the dissolution of the world's strongest economy.

In the days ahead I will propose removing the roadblocks that have slowed our economy and reduced productivity. Steps will be taken aimed at restoring the balance between the various levels of government. Progress may be slow, measured in inches and feet, not miles, but we will progress. It is time to reawaken this industrial giant, to get government back within its means, and to lighten our punitive tax burden. And these will be our first priorities, and on these principles there will be no compromise.

On the eve of our struggle for independence a man who might have been one of the greatest among the Founding Fathers, Dr. Joseph Warren, president of the Massachusetts Congress, said to his fellow Americans, "Our country is in danger, but not to be despaired of. . . . On you depend the fortunes of America. You are to decide the important questions upon which rests the happiness and the liberty of millions yet unborn. Act worthy of yourselves."

Well, I believe we, the Americans of today, are ready to act worthy of ourselves, ready to do what must be done to ensure happiness and liberty for ourselves, our children, and our children's children. And as we renew ourselves here in our own land, we will be seen as having greater strength throughout the world. We will again be the exemplar of freedom and a beacon of hope for those who do not now have freedom.

To those neighbors and allies who share our freedom, we will strengthen our historic ties and assure them of our support and firm commitment. We will match loyalty with loyalty. We will strive for mutually beneficial relations. We will not use our friendship to impose on their sovereignty, for our own sovereignty is not for sale.

As for the enemies of freedom, those who are potential adversaries, they will be reminded that peace is the highest aspiration of the American people. We will negotiate for it, sacrifice for it; we will not surrender for it, now or ever.

Our forbearance should never be misunderstood. Our reluctance for conflict should not be misjudged as a failure of will. When action is required to preserve our national security, we will act. We will maintain sufficient strength to prevail if need be, knowing that if we do so

155

we have the best chance of never having to use that strength.

Above all, we must realize that no arsenal or no weapon in the arsenals of the world is so formidable as the will and moral courage of free men and women. It is a weapon our adversaries in today's world do not have. It is a weapon that we as Americans do have. Let that be understood by those who practice terrorism and prey upon their neighbors.

I'm told that tens of thousands of prayer meetings are being held on this day, and for that I'm deeply grateful. We are a nation under God, and I believe God intended for us to be free. It would be fitting and good, I think, if on each Inaugural Day in future years it should be declared a day of prayer.

This is the first time in our history that this ceremony has been held, as you've been told, on this West Front of the Capitol. Standing here, one faces a magnificent vista, opening up on this city's special beauty and history. At the end of this open mall are those shrines to the giants on whose shoulders we stand.

Directly in front of me, the monument to a monumental man, George Washington, father of our country. A man of humility who came to greatness reluctantly. He led America out of revolutionary victory into infant nationhood. Off

156

to one side, the stately memorial to Thomas Jefferson. The Declaration of Independence flames with his eloquence. And then, beyond the Reflecting Pool, the dignified columns of the Lincoln Memorial. Whoever would understand in his heart the meaning of America will find it in the life of Abraham Lincoln.

Beyond those monuments to heroism is the Potomac River, and on the far shore the sloping hills of Arlington National Cemetery, with its row upon row of simple white markers bearing crosses or Stars of David. They add up to only a tiny fraction of the price that has been paid for our freedom.

Each one of those markers is a monument to the kind of hero I spoke of earlier. Their lives ended in places called Belleau Wood, The Argonne, Omaha Beach, Salerno, and halfway around the world on Guadalcanal, Tarawa, Pork Chop Hill, the Chosin Reservoir, and in a hundred rice paddies and jungles of a place called Vietnam.

Under one such marker lies a young man, Martin Treptow, who left his job in a small town barbershop in 1917 to go to France with the famed Rainbow Division. There, on the western front, he was killed trying to carry a message between battalions under heavy artillery fire.

We're told that on his body was found a diary. On the flyleaf under the heading, "My Pledge," he had written these words: "America must win this war. Therefore I will work, I will save, I will sacrifice, I will endure, I will fight cheerfully and do my utmost, as if the issue of the whole struggle depended on me alone."

The crisis we are facing today does not require of us the kind of sacrifice that Martin Treptow and so many thousands of others were called upon to make. It does require, however, our best effort and our willingness to believe in ourselves and to believe in our capacity to perform great deeds, to believe that together with God's help we can and will resolve the problems which now confront us.

And after all, why shouldn't we believe that? We are Americans.

God bless you, and thank you.

157

Address to the Republican National Convention, Houston, Texas, August 17, 1992

Thank you, Paul, for that kind introduction.

Mr. Chairman, delegates, friends, fellow Americans, thank you so very much for that welcome. You've given Nancy and me so many wonderful memories, so much of your warmth and affection. We cannot thank you enough for the honor of your friendship.

Over the years, I've addressed this convention as a private citizen, as a governor, as a Presidential candidate, as a President, and now, once again tonight, as private citizen Ronald Reagan. Tonight is a very special night for me. Of course, at my age, every night's a special night. After all, I was born in 1911.

Indeed, according to the experts I have exceeded my life expectancy by quite a few years. This is a source of great annoyance to some—especially to those in the Democratic Party.

But, here's the remarkable thing about being born in 1911. In my life's journey over these past eight decades, I have seen the human race through a period of unparalleled tumult and triumph. I have wit-

FAREWELL TO THE PARTY

nessed the bloody futility of two World Wars, Korea, Vietnam and the Persian Gulf. I have seen Germany united, divided, and united again. I have seen television grow from a parlor novelty to become the most powerful vehicle of communication in history. As a boy I saw streets filled with Model-Ts; as a man I have met men who walked on the moon.

I have not only seen, but lived the marvels of what historians have called the "American Century." Yet, tonight is not a time to look backward. For a while, I take inspiration from the past; like most Americans, I live for the future. So this evening, for just a few minutes, I hope you will let me talk about a country that is forever young.

* * *

There was a time when empires were defined by land mass, subjugated peoples, and military might. But the United States is unique because we are an empire of ideals. For two hundred years, we have been set apart by our faith in the ideals of Democracy, of free men and free markets, and of the extraordinary possibilities that lie within seemingly ordinary men and women. We believe that no power of government

158

is as formidable a force for good as the creativity and entrepreneurial drive of the American people.

Those are the ideals that invented revolutionary technologies and a culture envied by people everywhere. This powerful sense of energy has made America synonymous for opportunity the world over. And after generations of struggle, America is the moral force that defeated communism and all those who would put the human soul itself into bondage.

Within a few short years, we Americans have experienced the most sweeping changes of this century: The fall of the Soviet Union and the rise of the global economy. No transition is without its problems, but as uncomfortable as it may feel at the moment, the changes of the 1990s will leave America more dynamic and less in danger than at any time in my life.

A fellow named James Allen once wrote in his diary, "Many thinking people believe America has seen its best days." He wrote that on July 26, 1775. There are still those who believe America is weakening; that our glory was the brief flash of time called the 20th Century; that ours was a burst of greatness too bright and brilliant to sustain; that America's purpose is past.

My friends, I utterly reject those views. That's not the America

159

we know. We were meant to be masters of destiny, not victims of fate. Who among us would trade America's future for that of any other country in the world? And who could possibly have so little faith in our American people that they would trade our tomorrows for our yesterdays?

I'll give you a hint—They put on quite a production in New York a few weeks ago—you might even call it—slick.

A stone's throw from Broadway it was, and how appropriate.

Over and over they told us they are not the party they were. They kept telling us with a straight face that they're for family values. They're for a strong America. They're for a less intrusive government.

And they call me an actor!!!

To hear them talk, you'd never know that the nightmare of nuclear annihilation has been lifted from

our sleep. You'd never know that our standard of living remains the highest in the world. You'd never know that our air is cleaner than it was 20 years ago. You'd never know that we remain the one nation the rest of the world looks to for leadership.

It wasn't always this way. We mustn't forget—even if they would like to—the very different America that existed just twelve years ago; An America with 21 percent interest rates and back-to-back years of double-digit inflation; an America where mortgage payments doubled, paychecks plunged, and motorists sat in gas lines; an America of scarcity and sacrifice; and that what we really needed was another good dose of government control and higher taxes.

It wasn't so long ago that the world was a far more dangerous place as well. It was a world where aggressive Soviet communism was

on the rise and American strength was in decline. It was a world where our children came of age under the threat of nuclear holocaust. It was a world where our leaders told us that standing up to aggressors was dangerous—that American might and determination were somehow obstacles to peace.

But we stood tall and proclaimed that communism was destined for the ash-heap of history. We never heard so much ridicule from our liberal friends. The only thing that got them more upset was two simple words: "Evil Empire".

But we knew then what the liberal Democrat leaders just couldn't figure out: The sky would not fall if America restored her strength and resolve. The sky would not fall if an American President spoke the truth. The only thing that would fall was the Berlin Wall.

I heard those speakers at that

other convention saying, "We won the Cold War," and I couldn't help wondering, just who exactly do they mean by "We"?

And to top it off, they even tried to portray themselves as sharing the same fundamental values of our party!

But they truly don't understand the principle so eloquently stated by Abraham Lincoln: "You cannot strengthen the weak by weakening the strong. You cannot help the wage-earner by pulling down the wage-payer. You cannot help the poor by destroying the rich. You cannot help men permanently by doing for them what they could and should do for themselves."

If we ever hear the Democrats quoting that passage by Lincoln and acting like they mean it, then, my friends we see all that rhetorical smoke billowing out from the Democrats—well, ladies and gentle-men, I'd follow the example of their nominee—don't inhale.

This fellow they've nominated claims he's the new Thomas Jefferson. Well, let me tell you something … I knew Thomas Jefferson. He was a friend of mine … Governor, you're no Thomas Jefferson!!

Now let's not dismiss our current troubles, but where they see only problems, I see possibilities—as vast and diverse as the American Family itself. Even as we meet, the rest of the world is astounded by the pundits and fingerpointers who are so down on us as a nation.

Well I've said it before and I'll say it again—America's best days are yet to come. Our proudest moments are yet to be. Our most glorious achievements are just ahead.

America remains what Emerson called her 150 years ago, "The Country of Tomorrow." What a wonderful description and how true.

* * *

And yet tomorrow might never have happened had we lacked the courage of the 1980s to chart a course of strength and honor.

All the more reason no one should underestimate the importance of this campaign and what the outcome will mean. The stakes are high. The presidency is serious business. We cannot afford to take a chance. We need a man of serious purpose, unmatched experience, knowledge and ability. A man who understands government, who understands our country, and who understands the world. A man who has been at the table with Gorbachev and Yeltsin. A man whose performance as Commander-in-Chief of the bravest and most effective fighting force in history left the world in awe and the people of Kuwait free of foreign tyranny. A

161

man who has devoted more than half of his life to serving his country. A man of decency, integrity and honor.

And tonight I come to tell you that I—warmly, genuinely, whole-heartedly—support the re-election of George Bush as President of the United States.

We know President Bush. By his own admission, he is a quiet man, not a showman. He is a trustworthy and level-headed leader who is respected around the world. His is a steady hand on the tiller through the choppy waters of the 90s, which is exactly what we need.

We need George Bush!

We also need another real fighter—a man who happens to be with us this evening—someone who has repeatedly stood up for his deepest convictions. We need our Vice President, Dan Quayle.

Now it's true: A lot of liberal Democrats are saying it's time for a change; and they're right; the only trouble is they're pointing to the wrong end of Pennsylvania Avenue. What we should change is a Democratic Congress that wastes precious time on partisan matters of absolutely no relevance to the needs of the average American. So to all the entrenched interests along the Potomac—the gavel-wielding chair-men, the bloated staffs, the taxers and takers and congressional rule-makers, we have a simple slogan for November 1992: Clean House!

For you see, my fellow Republicans, we are the change! For 50 of the last 60 years the Democrats have controlled the Senate. And they've had the House of Representatives for 56 of the last 60 years.

It's time to clean house. Clean out the privileges and perks. Clean out the arrogance and the big egos.

Clean out the scandals, the corner-cutting and the foot-dragging.

What kind of job do you think they've done during all those years they've been running the Congress?

You know, I used to say to some of those Democrats who chair every committee in the House: "You need to balance the government's check-book the same way you balance your own." Then I learned how they ran the House bank, and I realized that was exactly what they had been doing.

Now, just imagine what they would do if they controlled the Executive Branch, too!

This is the 21st Presidential election in my lifetime, the 16th in which I will cast a ballot. Each of those elections had its shifting moods of the moment, its headlines of one day that were forgotten the next. There have been a few more twists and turns this year than in others, a little more shouting about who was up or down, in or out, as we went about selecting our candidates. But now we have arrived, as we always do, at the moment of truth—the serious business of selecting a President.

Now is the time for choosing.

As it did twelve years ago, and as we have seen many times in history, our country now stands at a crossroads. There is widespread doubt about our public institutions and profound concern, not merely about the economy but about the overall direction of this great country.

* * *

And as they did then, the American people are clamoring for change and sweeping reform. The question we had to ask twelve years ago is the question we ask today: What kind of change can we Republicans offer the American people?

Some might believe that the things we have talked about tonight are irrelevant to the choice. These new isolationists claim that the American people don't care about how or why we prevailed over our adversaries. They insist that our triumph is yesterday's news, part of a past that holds no lessons for the future.

Well nothing could be more tragic, after having come all this way on the journey of renewal we began 12 years ago, than if America herself forgot the lessons of individual liberty that she has taught to a grateful world.

Emerson was right. We are the country of tomorrow, our revolution did not end at Yorktown. More than two centuries later, America remains on a voyage of discovery, a land that has never become, but is always in the act of becoming.

But just as we have led the crusade for democracy beyond our shores, we have a great task to do together in our own home. Now, I would appeal to you to invigorate democracy in your own neighborhoods.

Whether we come from poverty or wealth; whether we are Afro-American or Irish-American; Christian or Jewish, from big cities or small towns, we are all equal in the eyes of God. But as Americans that is not enough—we must be equal in the eyes of each other. We can no longer judge each other on the basis of what we are, but must, instead, start finding out who we are. In America, our origins matter less than our destinations and that is what democracy is all about.

A decade after we summoned America to a new beginning, we are beginning still. Every day brings fresh challenges and opportunities to match. With each sunrise we

163

are reminded that millions of our citizens have yet to share in the abundance of American prosperity. Many languish in neighborhoods riddled with drugs and bereft of hope. Still others hesitate to venture out on the streets for fear of criminal violence. Let us pledge ourselves to a new beginning for them.

Let us apply our ingenuity and remarkable spirit to revolutionize education in America so that everyone among us will have the mental tools to build a better life. And while we do so, let's remember that the most profound education begins in the home.

164

And let us harness the competitive energy that built America, into rebuilding our inner cities so that real jobs can be created for those who live there and real hope can rise out of despair.

Let us strengthen our health

care system so that Americans of all ages can be secure in their futures without the fear of financial ruin. And my friends, once and for all, let us get control of the federal deficit through a balanced budget amendment and line item veto.

And let us all renew our commitment—renew our pledge to day-by-day, person-by-person, make our country and the world a better place to live. Then, when the nations of the world turn to us and say, "America, you are the model of freedom and prosperity," we can turn to them and say, "You ain't seen nothing, yet!"

For me, tonight is the latest chapter in a story that began a quarter of a century ago, when the people of California entrusted me with the stewardship of their dreams.

My fellow citizens—those of you here in this hall and those of you at home—I want you to know that I have always had the highest respect for you, for your common sense and intelligence and for your decency. I have always believed in you and in what you could accomplish for yourselves and for others.

And whatever else history may say about me when I'm gone, I hope it will record that I appealed to your best hopes, not your worst fears, to your confidence rather than your doubts. My dream is that you will travel the road ahead with liberty's lamp guiding your steps and opportunity's arm steadying your way.

My fondest hope for each one of you—and especially for the young people here—is that you will love your country, not for her power or wealth, but for her self-lessness and her idealism. May each of you have the heart to con-ceive, the understanding to direct, and the hand to execute works that will make the world a little better for your having been here.

May all of you as Americans never forget your heroic origins, never fail to seek divine guidance, and never lose your natural, God-given optimism.

And finally, my fellow Americans, may every dawn be a great new beginning for America and every evening bring us closer to that shining city upon a hill.

Before I go, I would like to ask the person who has made my life's journey so meaningful, someone I have been so very proud of over the years to join me … Nancy.

My fellow Americans, on behalf of both of us, goodbye, God bless each and every one of you, and God bless this country we love.

165

Transcript of a hand-written letter from President Ronald Reagan to the American People, November 5, 1994

I have recently been told that I am one of the millions of Americans who will be afflicted with Alzheimer's Disease.

Upon learning this news, Nancy and I had to decide whether as private citizens we would keep this a private matter or whether we would make this news known in a public way.

In the past, Nancy suffered from breast cancer and I had my cancer surgeries. We found through our open disclosures we were able to raise public awareness. We were happy that, as a result, many more people underwent testing. They were treated in early stages and able to return to normal, healthy lives.

So now, we feel it is important to share it with you. In opening our hearts, we hope this might promote greater awareness of this condition. Perhaps it will encourage a clearer understanding of the individuals and families who are affected by it.

At the moment I feel just fine. I intend to live the remainder of the

THE COUNTRY I LOVE

years God gives me on this earth doing the things I have always done. I will continue to share life's journey with my beloved Nancy and my family. I plan to enjoy the great outdoors and stay in touch with my friends and supporters.

Unfortunately, as Alzheimer's Disease progresses, the family often bears a heavy burden. I only wish there was some way I could spare Nancy from this painful experience. When the time comes, I am confident that with your help she will face it with faith and courage.

In closing, let me thank you, the American people, for giving me the great honor of allowing me to serve as your President. When the Lord calls me home, whenever that may be, I will leave with the greatest love for this country of ours and eternal optimism for its future.

I now begin the journey that will lead me into the sunset of my life. I know that for America there will always be a bright dawn ahead.

Thank you, my friends. May God always bless you.

Sincerely,

Ronald Reagan

167

Ronald Reagan loved the truth. We all do or say we do, but Reagan thought the truth uniquely constructive. He thought that just by voicing it one could actually begin to make things better. He thought that the truth was the only foundation on which something strong and good and even towering could be built. He thought that in politics and world affairs of his time there had been too many lies for too long, and that they had been uniquely destructive.

Reagan's public career was to counter that destructiveness by speaking the truth, spreading it, and repeating it. He wanted to put words into the air that were honest and have them take the place of other words in the air that were not.

That is why he called the Soviet Union "the locus of evil in the modern world." It shocked people when he said it, and not because it wasn't or didn't seem to be or couldn't possibly be true. It shocked people because it wasn't the kind of thing that was said in public, or even for some people in private. But Reagan thought honest words set the predicate for honest deeds and effective diplomacy.

Reagan knew, as Churchill did, that democracy is the least perfect form of government, except for all the others. So he said it. Reagan also quoted Lincoln to the effect that no man is superior enough to claim the right to rule another man without the other's consent. He

Afterword

believed in the common wisdom of the man and woman on the American streets, and would listen to them and laud them before he would do either with the intelligentsia—or those he still thought of as eggheads. He thought that if they were so smart they wouldn't all think the same things, that there would be more diversity among them, more questioning. He once told me that a lot of intellectuals have a Phi Beta Kappa key on one end of the chain and no watch on the other. "They never know what time it is." His attitude toward those who admire themselves was also skeptical. He would sometimes tell of the big economic study that was done on the U.S. economy in the decades just after the turn of the last century. It was long and comprehensive and was unveiled with great fanfare. It had given a lot of attention to various trends and realities, but it had overlooked the fantastic rise of electronic media, which would soon transform the American marketplace. One got the sense that he thought if they'd only talked to a lowly technician working for General Sarnoff they wouldn't have missed the obvious. Reagan thought that's what elites were for: to miss the obvious.

* * *

More truth, according to Reagan: Thoreau was right when he said, "That government is best which governs least." Governments consist of concentrated areas of power held by humans, and groups of humans holding concentrated power will always cause mischief. The liberals of the Reagan era thought that only government can be trusted to look out for all the people. But Reagan thought not: Government, he said, tends to look out for government, to mold citizens to meet its needs rather than mold itself to meet theirs. Therefore, the citizenry must limit the size and scope of power given to government, and err on the side of caution.

Reagan thought there is a God who is good; he thought America is and was from the beginning exceptional, something new in the history of man, because it was founded on ideas, beautiful and true ones that advanced human liberty.

And so his stands: Make government smaller, lower taxes, leave the people as much of their money as possible, protect their autonomy. Allow religious faith a wide and healthy dome in which to breathe. Define the difference between

democracy and totalitarianism, and show how history proves that the former is most likely to keep the peace and increase well-being. Stay strong in the face of those who would harm democracy, who would set back freedom and do damage to the world.

All of these questions and issues and ideas brought him into politics. And what he thought, how he thought, didn't change. The immature are always finding new truths, the cynical are always discovering new philosophies to claim to believe in. Reagan was neither immature nor cynical, and so his consistency, which would have been impressive in anybody, was truly stunning in a politician.

* * *

You know who knew firsthand the power of truth in helping the world? Anatoly Shcharansky.

I keep on the wall of my office a faded newspaper clipping framed in old glass. The headline is "Reagan Talks Hailed in Gulag." The subhead: "Dissident Says Speeches Inspired Political Inmates." The story was about what Shcharansky, the newly free Soviet political prisoner, told President Reagan when he met with him shortly after being freed from the Soviet Union. Shcharansky told Reagan that his hard-line anti-communist speeches were so admired by the inmates of Soviet forced-labor camps that snippets of news about them were secretly communicated from cell to cell. He said that prisoners sometimes learned of Reagan's statements through Soviet news reports intended to inflame the public against the President. But the news had the opposite effect in the gulag. Reagan's words were very helpful, he said, and that is why they were passed from cell to cell. "There are ways of communicating in the cells, even the punishment cells," Shcharansky had been quoted as saying.

* * *

Ronald Reagan's time in the White House was uniquely constructive. He unleashed the economic boom that almost 20 years later continues to echo throughout the country and the world. He began his tenure in the White House predicting the end of Soviet totalitarianism—he said it would be consigned "to the ash heap of history"—and by the time he left the White House he was helping to oversee its demise. And nine months after he left the White House for the last time as President, the Berlin Wall came down.

What an era, what a presidency, what a great moment in human history. It was only 20 years ago that it

171

began, and yet those of us who worked for and with Reagan, when we see each other across a room or bump into one another at a symposium, we look like we are veterans of an old war. We lock eyes, say "How you doin'?" and then we throw ourselves in each others' arms and laugh and say, "Still here, kid." We talk about those we worked with, decisions that got made, and we say, "Have you seen the old man?" These days that question is followed with a shake of the head and a movement of the hands that says "a little better" or "a little worse." And we talk about who Reagan was in history, and who he was as a human being.

I found something that reminds me of him, that captures him for me. It's from Stephen Vincent Benét's epic prose poem on the Civil War, *John Brown's Body.*

Sometimes there comes a crack in Time itself.
Sometimes the earth is torn by something blind.
Sometimes an image that has stood so long
It seems implanted as the polar star
Is moved against an unfathomed force
That suddenly will not have it any more.

Call it the mores, call it God or Fate,
Call it Mansoul or economic law,
That force exists and moves.

       And when it moves
It will employ a hard and actual stone
To batter into bits an actual wall
And change the actual scheme of things.

I think Ronald Reagan was a hard and actual stone who battered into bits an actual wall. He did it with many others and in many ways, but one way, a big one, was with words, with which he deployed that most constructive thing—the truth.

Peggy Noonan

172

We looked forward to this project because we knew it would let us consider a vital contemporary question: During an era in which three of the past five Presidents failed at the ballot box, a fourth left office in scandal, and the outlook for the current presidency remains uncertain, at best, what caused the success of the presidency of Ronald Reagan?

The answer, we found, is as simple as the truths underlying virtually every word in this book: candor; humor; respect for each individual as God's special, equal creation, grounded in an intense personal faith; and an unswerving commitment to conservative principles.

As we celebrate the 20th anniversary of Ronald Reagan's inauguration as President launching the "Reagan Revolution," and the recognition of his historic contribution to America and the world, his words and legacy are more compelling than ever to those who share his optimism about the greatness of America. We hope these words will help a few more individuals share that optimism.

Erik Felten
Paul Wilkinson

RESEARCHERS' NOTE